Sunset

Waterwise Gardening

By the Editors of Sunset Books and Sunset Magazine

Undemanding goldmoss sedum (Sedum acre).

Sunset Publishing Corporation ■ Menlo Park, California

Bougainvillea 'Barbara Karst' cascades down wall.

Book Editors
Fran Feldman
Cornelia Fogle

Research & Text
Kathryn Stechert Black
John R. Dunmire
Philip Edinger
Joseph F. Williamson

Coordinating Editor
Gregory J. Kaufman

Design
Joe di Chiarro

Illustrations
Mary Davey Burkhardt
Jane McCreary

Maps
Rik Olson

Unthirsty Gardens

At one time or another, all parts of the country have experienced extended dry periods, whether occurring naturally, as in the West during the summer, or as quirks of nature.

That's why water-thrifty gardens make so much sense. Don't think of them merely as expanses of gravel with a tree here and there. As you'll learn in this book, waterwise gardens offer an amazing diversity of colors, textures, shapes, and sizes. What distinguishes them from traditional landscapes is their adherence to some basic principles: good design, careful choice and placement of plants, little or no turf, efficient watering systems, and water-conserving maintenance practices.

Glance through these pages— you'll find colorful photos of splendid water-thrifty gardens; detailed information on how to plant, water, and care for your plants; and a comprehensive listing of those plants that, when used in appropriate climates, get along well with little or no watering.

We are grateful to the following water district personnel, landscape architects and designers, and plant experts who helped with the preparation of the manuscript: Bruce Adams, Regula Campbell, Brenda Chapman, Ali Davidson, Steve Domigan, Randall Ismay, Erik Katzmaier, Martha Latta, Randy Lewis, John Nelson, Marsha Prillwitz, Liz Seymour, Steve Trudnak, and Anne K. Young.

We also thank Lynne Tremble for scouting some of the photo situations.

Cover: Unthirsty plants bring vibrant spring color to this coastal garden. Blooming varieties include, from top, tall purple spires of Pride of Madeira (Echium fastuosum), dark blue Ceanothus 'Julia Phelps', yellow Canary Island broom (Cytisus canariensis), and lilac-colored sea lavender (Limonium perezii). In foreground, at left, is Euryops pectinatus. Cover design by Susan Bryant. Photography by Norman A. Plate.

Photographers: Glenn Christiansen, 31, 50; Derek Fell, 1, 59 (left); Mark E. Gibson, 58 (left); Saxon Holt, 16; Horticultural Photography, 61 (left); Michael Landis, 8, 13; Ells Marugg, 20, 58 (right); Don Normark, 23 (bottom), 57 (right); Norman A. Plate, 2, 21, 23 (top), 26, 27, 60 (right); Bill Ross, 14, 15, 19, 25 (top), 54, 56 (right), 57 (left), 62 (right); Chad Slattery, 9, 10, 18, 64; Bill Stephens, 34; David Stubbs, 24, 28; Jeff Teeter, 60 (left); Michael S. Thompson, 59 (bottom center), 61 (right); Peter O. Whiteley, 4, 17; Russ Widstrand, 25 (bottom), 30, 56 (left); Tom Wyatt, 40, 43, 48, 59 (top right, bottom right), 62 (left).

Editor, Sunset Books: Elizabeth L. Hogan

Third printing March 1991

Contents

Special Features

Water— A Precious Resource

Beyond the plants you grow, the three other essential components of gardening are water, sunlight, and soil. This book deals with what may be the most crucial variable in your garden's environment, water.

The amount of precipitation that falls on an area in the course of a year varies all over this globe; it varies considerably just within the United States. And if you garden, the amount of water that nature gives you makes an immense difference in what you grow and how you grow it.

Generally speaking, the eastern half of the United States has always received enough—sometimes too much—precipitation. But, for various reasons, regions within this area can sometimes go several years without getting enough water to supply the needs of the people who live there.

That "generally-gets-enough-water" area runs from the Atlantic Ocean west across the Mississippi and Missouri rivers to a north-south line that comes very close to being the 100th meridian (or 100° west longitude). As you can see on the map on page 6, that particular longitude line runs through the middle of Texas (near Abilene), forms the eastern base of the panhandle of Oklahoma, runs through western Kansas, and continues up through the middle of Nebraska, South Dakota, and North Dakota. As you approach this line, proceeding from east to west, rainfall becomes gradually chancier.

West of that line, aridity is the basis of agriculture and gardening. In most of the low elevations of Washington, Oregon, and California, the limited water picture takes on another special char-

Hillside garden hosts flourishing low-water-use plants. Prominent flowers are pink Peruvian verbena (Verbena peruviana) and purple sea lavender (Limonium perezii). Other color includes yellow coreopsis, white rockrose (Cistus), and gray-leafed snow-in-summer (Cerastium tomentosum). Landscape architect: Nancy Hardesty.

acteristic: almost all of the precipitation occurs between late fall of one year and late spring of the next.

In other, generally higher elevations, precipitation is scattered, to some degree, around the calendar; even so, it doesn't add up to the evenly distributed, green-grass-in-summer kind of precipitation that takes place east of the 100th meridian, as shown in the charts on the facing page.

Droughts

Droughts—of months or years in duration—occasionally descend on areas all over the United States. A drought is a period of time during which a region gets less than what is considered normal precipitation. The word has been, and probably always will be, more appropriate in the East and Midwest than in the Far West.

In the Midwest and East, historically, every dry period has ended with the return of adequate rainfall. Such a period, with a beginning and an end, is a drought. But in the permanently arid West, the land is forever in a state of inadequate precipitation for local needs, so the midwestern and eastern sense of the word "drought," as a temporary ab-

normal condition, is inappropriate in the West.

In the heavily populated regions of the arid West, water is imported, usually over considerable distances, by pipelines and canals from reservoirs fed by rivers that are, themselves, fed by mountain streams. These populated areas depend on distant wintertime snowfall and rainfall for their supply of water. In years when precipitation is lower than normal and those reservoirs cannot provide adequate amounts of water, gardeners in the irrigated arid areas must turn to especially broad forms of water thriftiness.

Rainfall Amounts Between May 1 & October 31

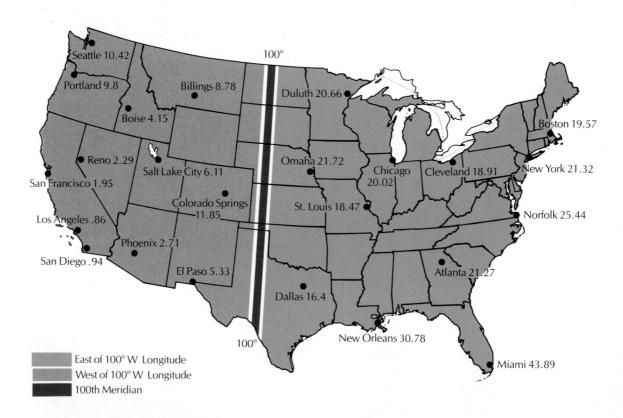

Numbers on the map show the average number of inches of rain each of the indicated cities receives between May 1 and October 31. Together, the numbers clearly show how much drier the West is than the East during that half of the year. Over those critical six months, the 12 weather stations shown on the map west of the 100th meridian typically receive from .86 inch to 11.85 inches of rain. During the same period, none of the 12 weather stations east of that line gets less than 16.4 inches—and the wettest gets 43.89.

What Is a Waterwise Garden?

Elsewhere in this book you'll read in detail about the ways you can get the most from your garden on a limited amount of water. The seven fundamental principles outlined below, used as a group, provide the basis for a successful waterwise garden.

Planning and design. The idea here is to lay out your garden so that it will use water as efficiently as possible, zoning plants so you have the big water users together where you can water them without waste, and placing the lighter water-using plants together elsewhere, where irrigation will be minimal or unnecessary.

It's best to begin with a master plan that takes into account all landscape elements; this also allows you to install your landscape in phases, if desired. You can create your own design or work with a landscape professional. A landscape contractor or other installation specialist can help you with the work of installing your garden.

Limited turf areas. One big message is clear: a lawn uses four times as much water as anything else in landscaping; so if you live in an arid-summer region (see map on facing page), you shouldn't bother at all with a lawn unless you need it for recreational activities or some other specific purpose. For such uses, keep only as much lawn as your activities really require.

In regions that get more than 2 inches of rain per month from May through October, it's fairly easy to keep a lawn because nature usually waters it for you. In regions that get less than 2 inches a month from May through October, a lawn must be watered all summer or it will die.

Cities West of 100° W Longitude

CITY	INCHES OF RAIN, AVERAGE							
	May	**June**	**July**	**August**	**September**	**October**	**May–October**	**Full year**
Los Angeles	.23	.03	.00	.12	.27	.21	.86	14.85
San Diego	.24	.06	.01	.11	.19	.33	.94	9.32
San Francisco	.35	.15	.04	.08	.24	1.09	1.95	19.33
Reno	.74	.34	.30	.27	.30	.34	2.29	7.49
Phoenix	.14	.17	.74	1.02	.64	.63	2.71	7.11
Boise	1.21	.95	.26	.40	.58	.75	4.15	11.71
El Paso	.24	.56	1.60	1.21	1.42	.70	5.33	7.82
Salt Lake City	1.47	.97	.72	.92	.89	1.14	6.11	15.31
Billings	2.39	2.07	.85	1.05	1.26	1.16	8.78	15.09
Portland	2.08	1.47	.46	1.13	1.61	3.05	9.80	37.39
Seattle	1.58	1.38	.74	1.27	2.02	3.43	10.42	38.60
Colorado Springs	2.28	2.02	2.85	2.61	1.31	.78	11.85	15.42

Cities East of 100° W Longitude

CITY	INCHES OF RAIN, AVERAGE							
	May	**June**	**July**	**August**	**September**	**October**	**May–October**	**Full year**
Dallas	4.27	2.59	2.00	1.76	3.31	2.47	16.40	29.45
St. Louis	3.54	3.73	3.63	2.55	2.70	2.32	18.47	33.91
Cleveland	3.30	3.49	3.37	3.38	2.92	2.45	18.91	35.40
Boston	3.52	2.92	2.68	3.68	3.41	3.36	19.57	43.81
Chicago	3.15	4.08	3.63	3.53	3.35	2.28	20.02	33.34
Duluth	3.15	3.96	3.96	4.12	3.26	2.21	20.66	29.68
Atlanta	4.02	3.91	4.73	3.41	3.17	2.53	21.27	48.61
New York	3.46	3.15	3.67	4.32	3.48	3.24	21.32	42.82
Omaha	4.33	4.08	3.62	4.10	3.50	2.09	21.72	30.34
Norfolk	3.75	3.45	5.15	5.33	4.35	3.41	25.44	45.22
New Orleans	5.07	4.63	6.73	6.02	5.67	2.66	30.78	59.74
Miami	6.53	9.15	5.98	7.02	8.07	7.14	43.89	57.55

Efficient irrigation. Make sure that your watering practices and devices use water as thriftily as possible. Today, there are water-efficient application systems for every kind of garden planting: trees, shrubs, ground covers, lawns, vine and bush crops, flowers and vegetables planted in rows, and flowers and vegetables planted in masses.

A well-planned watering system can help you avoid overwatering, which not only wastes water but can be a cause of plant death and disease.

The two most efficient water-delivery systems are underground sprinklers and drip irrigation. You can use a hose-end sprinkler, but you'll have to pay close attention to placement. A controller, or timer, that regulates the amount of time you water is an essential element of any waterwise garden.

Soil improvements. The gardener's traditional, everlasting marriage to the soil—routinely cultivating it and incorporating organic matter into it—constantly increases that soil's ability to conserve water.

Mulches. When you put certain kinds of organic or mineral materials over soil or under and around existing crops, you greatly reduce the moisture loss through evaporation. Mulches also can reduce the growth of weeds and help slow erosion.

Moreover, mulches provide landscape interest, as shown in the photograph below, and can be ideal alternatives to turf. Typical organic mulches are wood by-products, such as aged sawdust and shredded bark, peat moss, animal manures, and commercially prepared composts. Common inorganic ones are rock and gravel.

Low-water-use plants. By their evolutionary inheritance, some plants must have a lot of water in order to survive; others perform quite well with very limited water. As you select your permanent plants, you'd be wise to choose as few as possible of the heavy water consumers.

You'll find low-water-use trees, shrubs, flowering plants, ground covers, and even some grasses. Some provide seasonal colors, others year-round green. The key is to choose those that are well adapted to your region.

Appropriate maintenance. Haphazard garden maintenance can and does waste millions of gallons of water a year. Waterwise gardening means paying attention. It means faucets don't drip; sprinkler and drip systems work with maximum efficiency; watering is done when plants need it, and not by the clock or the calendar; above-ground irrigation takes place when the air is quiet so wind doesn't evaporate the water and waste it; and watering is controlled to avoid that most intolerable water-waster, runoff.

Because weeds, like all other plants, consume water, it's essential to keep them under control by hoeing, by pulling them up by hand, or by applying a herbicide. Then use a mulch to prevent them from returning.

Other waterwise maintenance chores, such as fertilizing and pruning, should only be done on an "as needed" basis.

Small circle of turf offers just enough play space for children; shape makes it easy to irrigate efficiently. Mulch and unthirsty ground covers and shrubs provide color and texture. Landscape designer: Alan Rollinger.

Intense yellow blooms of blue palo verde (Cercidium floridum), an especially low-water-use tree, strike a handsome silhouette against deep blue of midspring sky. Landscape architect: Marcus Bollinger.

Planning & Design

If the idea of a low-water-use landscape conjures up visions of gravel and meager plantings, reconsider, because a garden most certainly can be beautiful without being thirsty.

A successful waterwise garden uses limited water not because it skimps on plantings but because it makes wise plant choices and wise use of plants. It also creatively employs *hardscape,* which is everything in the garden that doesn't grow—decks, patios, walkways, fences, and more.

All flourishing waterwise gardens begin with careful planning, based on the principle of conserving water through creative landscaping. This type of gardening is called Xeriscaping, a word derived from the Greek *xeros,* meaning dry, combined with landscaping. The seven principles of Xeriscaping are explained on pages 7–8.

As you plan your waterwise garden, keep those practices, discussed here and in the following chapters, in mind. During the planning stage, you may wish to refer to the later chapters if you have specific questions about soil preparation, watering systems, or good maintenance practices.

Basic Design Principles

The two most important design elements for a successful waterwise garden are grouping plants of like needs together and either eliminating turf or keeping the amount of turf you plant to a practical size—as much as you need and no more. Both of these will result in considerable water savings.

Other important principles that landscape architects use in designing are unity, proportion, balance, variety, and color.

Bright display of purple verbena adds color to green acacias and agave in this desert garden. In background, littleleaf palo verde (Cercidium microphyllum) is in full bloom. Landscape designer: Margaret West.

Zoning the Landscape

By organizing your yard into zones, you can give each area the appropriate amount of water, avoiding the waste that comes from overdosing low-water-use plants placed near water-loving ones. You also ensure that every plant gets the environment—sun or shade— that suits it best.

In planning a waterwise garden, think of each area of your landscape as falling into a zone. Your specific site will determine how many zones you have, how much space each zone occupies, and how often each appears. An example of a zoned landscape is shown below.

Low-water-use zone. This is the area of lowest water need. Irrigation is used here only when new plants are added. Once they're established, which can take

as long as a year, the plants in this zone require little, if any, additional water. This is where wildflower seeds might be scattered or existing native vegetation would be preserved, if that suited the garden's style.

Moderate-water-use zone. Plants in this area require a bit more water than nature provides. That extra moisture can often be supplied by taking advantage of rain runoff from downspouts, driveways, and terraces. During very dry or hot periods, however, supplemental irrigation may be needed.

High-water-use zone. This is the place for the thirstiest plantings, which generally are turf, annual flower beds, vegetable gardens, and other water-loving plants. Cutting back on the size of this zone does the most to reduce water use.

Especially in the desert Southwest, "oasis" is the word used to apply to the high water zone. Generally, this small, lush zone in the midst of an arid landscape is placed next to the house where it can be enjoyed the most and where it's likely to suffer the least evaporation from wind and sun. In hot climates, an oasis placed next to the house also serves to cool it.

Limiting Turf Areas

No matter where you live, a lawn requires constant upkeep—mowing, weeding, fertilizing, and so on—as well as a great deal of water. Where rainfall is plentiful throughout the warm-weather season, a lawn is fairly easy to grow. But where summer water is scarce or nonexistent, such as in the arid-summer

Zoning a Desert Landscape

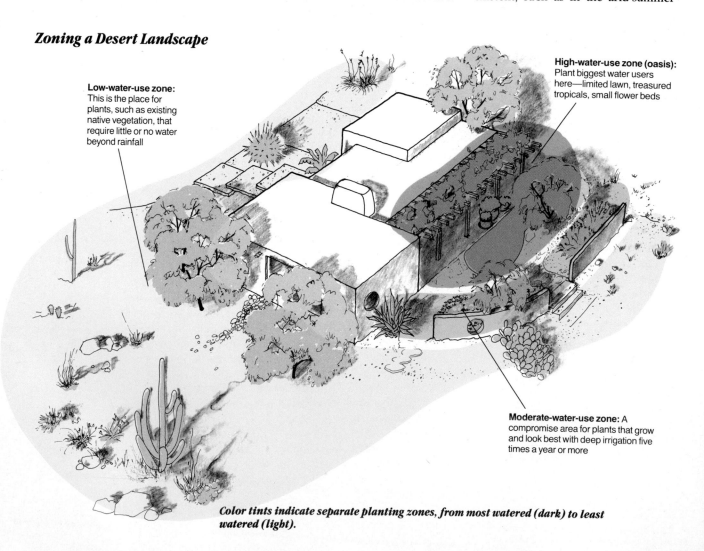

Low-water-use zone: This is the place for plants, such as existing native vegetation, that require little or no water beyond rainfall

High-water-use zone (oasis): Plant biggest water users here—limited lawn, treasured tropicals, small flower beds

Moderate-water-use zone: A compromise area for plants that grow and look best with deep irrigation five times a year or more

Color tints indicate separate planting zones, from most watered (dark) to least watered (light).

Small circle of high-water-use turf offers just enough play surface for children. Grass is tall fescue, a drought-tolerant variety. Landscape designer: Charlene Yockum.

West, a small lawn—or no lawn at all—makes especially good sense.

The major advantage of a lawn is that it supplies a comfortable and inviting surface for barefoot play and lounging on warm days. It also combines handsomely and easily with other garden textures and colors.

A lawn, however, doesn't have to be big to look good or be useful. Small lawns, in fact, can have a stronger total visual impact than large, expansive ones. And certainly, as you begin to consider alternatives to turf areas, it becomes clear that there are many forms of landscape beauty other than a large, mowed lawn.

Turf guidelines. When evaluating how much water-hungry turf you want in your garden, look to function first. If hardscape or other plants will do the job better, choose them instead.

Some landscape experts recommend that no more than 25 percent of a garden be given to turf. Others say that for most family activities, 600 to 800 square feet of lawn is plenty. But because each family's requirements are different, it's best to examine your own specific needs to determine lawn size and location.

For the turf areas you do have, keep these water-saving guidelines in mind as you plan:

■ *Choose the grass type carefully.* Look for the newer grass varieties that are attractive, tough, and use less water than traditional Kentucky bluegrass.

■ *Place the lawn where it will be most useful.* If the front yard is never used, consider ground cover or other plantings for it.

■ *Edge the lawn's perimeters* with wood or masonry strips for easier mowing.

■ *Avoid planting* low-water-use trees or shrubs in water-guzzling turf areas.

■ *Keep the physical layout* of the turf areas to easily irrigated shapes. A circle of turf usually works well. Avoid narrow strips of turf (less than 8 feet wide); they can't be watered efficiently.

■ *Consider placing beds* of thirsty annuals or vegetables near the turf areas so they'll benefit from the extra water applied there.

■ *Don't plant grass on steep slopes* where water runoff and soil erosion will be problems.

Alternatives to turf. Instead of grass, you can select unthirsty ground covers or creative hardscape, such as pavers or decking.

■ *Plants.* When you want a lawn only for its visual appeal—an expanse of green or a pretty setting, as is so often the case with the front yard—you may find you can substitute ground covers for an equally beautiful result. You can even walk on some ground cover plants, and most control erosion well.

In the front of your house, low shrubs and ground covers create an informal, woodsy look; hedges give a more formal appearance. All can provide pleasing, cooling texture and color, adding more interest and variety than a lawn.

■ *Hardscape.* Wood, stone, gravel, and other hardscape materials contrast attractively with planted areas at the same time that they perform a real function in the landscape. Try to select materials that both meet your needs and allow rain to penetrate the soil. Decks, for example, shade the soil and permit what rain you get to drip down between the boards. They also provide an excellent surface for entertaining, playing, or lounging.

Crushed rock, gravel, bark, wood chips, and bricks laid in sand also let rain soak through. And they have other advantages: they're attractive, relatively cheap, and widely available. All these materials also keep the soil cool, thereby reducing evaporation.

For more information about choosing plant and hardscape materials, turn to "Designing Your Garden" on page 20.

Other Design Considerations

When designing your landscape, it's important to aim for overall harmony within the garden and between the garden and its surroundings. Whether you're planning a large, formal landscape or something more modest, observing basic landscaping principles will ensure that your entire garden is visually pleasing.

Unity. A unified landscape is all of one piece, rather than disjointed groupings and scattered features. No one element stands out; instead, all the parts—plants and hardscape—work together.

Strong, observable lines and the repetition of geometric shapes contribute significantly to the unity of your landscape, as does simplicity—for example, using just a few harmonious colors and a limited number of plant varieties. Be prepared to give up the idea of having every one of your favorite plants around you and avoid designing too many distinct units that will have to be tied together.

As you plan, you may find it best to design a unified background first—a deck, perhaps. Think of this background as a neutral element around which you'll assemble your landscaping units. Just remember that the more separate elements you have, the harder it will be to achieve unity.

Proportion. In a well-designed landscape, the various structural and plant elements are in scale with one another. Start with your house; it will determine proportion in your landscape.

When choosing trees and shrubs, keep their ultimate sizes and shapes in mind. Though a tree when young may suit your front yard, it could overwhelm your house as it matures.

Balance. To balance a landscape is to use mass, color, or form to create equal visual weight on either side of a center of interest. In a formal landscape, balance may mean simply creating one side as a mirror image of the other.

In informal styles, balance is just as important, but more subtle: a large tree to the left of an entryway can be balanced by a grouping of smaller trees on the right. Likewise, you can balance a concentration of color in a small flower bed on one side of a patio with a much larger and more diffuse mass of greenery on the other side.

Variety. Break up a monotonous landscape by selecting plants in a variety of shapes, shades, and textures. Or add interest by juxtaposing different hardscape materials.

In just 7 years, water-guzzling landscape shown at top was transformed into water-saving one pictured at bottom. Expansive lawn in old garden provided little protection from wide-open exposure to street. New garden encloses house, creating a private outdoor gardening space. Photo in middle shows progress just 2 years after planting. For another view, see facing page.

Front yard is organized into three zones, each with its own intended use and its own watering system. Almost all plants are self-sufficient, with most drought-tolerant ones farthest from house. Lemon tree in center is surrounded by ground morning glory (Convolvulus mauritanicus) and other flowering plantings. White fortnight lilies (Dietes vegeta) sparkle at lower right.

Harmonious color scheme relies on variations of just three colors. Foliage ranges from green to gray green to gray blue. Rosy shades of used brick paving are echoed in pink-flowered common thrift (Armeria maritima), a low-growing ground cover. Landscape designer: Konrad Gauder of Landsculpture.

Visualize the combined appearance of plants and structural elements. Careful planning will help you avoid color clashes, the monotony of uniform leaf colors or textures, or a jumbled appearance resulting from a haphazard assortment of plant shapes and sizes.

Consider also the landscape views from inside the house. Perhaps you'll want a focal point outside the window of a favorite sitting room. Or you may want to choose low-growing plants in a certain area in order to preserve an especially striking view from a window.

Color. Although color is a consideration when you're striving for unity, balance, and variety, there are some special waterwise guidelines for using color.

When planning, try to select permanent plants—generally the less thirsty ones—that have varied and interesting foliage, bark, or blossoms.

Include in your plans ways to make the most of any annual color—likely to be high-water-use plants—that you may want to add. Give those few well-chosen plants center stage by planting them where you'll enjoy them most, such as beside an entryway or garden path, in a patio bed, or outside a window.

Clustering plants of the same color is another way to get the greatest impact from them. For help in choosing plants with seasonal color, see pages 56–57.

Evaluating Your Landscape

Before you draw up a plan or pick up a shovel, determine how you'll use your outdoor space and what functions you want your garden to perform. Then take a close look at your site to see how its special features affect your plans.

Determining Your Needs

A successful waterwise garden not only helps you conserve water but also meets your needs. If you're remodeling, you're probably already aware of how you want to use your garden. If you're starting fresh, this is a good time to consider what you want your ideal garden to look like.

Function. At the outset, decide what your garden's purpose will be. Will you use the space for outdoor activities, or will it mainly have a visual purpose?

Think about the outdoor activities you and your family enjoy, such as gardening, sunning, lawn games, and socializing. Determine whether you want to make room for such practical areas as a garden center for potting and tending plants or a storage space for firewood, garbage cans, or a recreational vehicle.

Consider traffic patterns to and from the house so you'll know where to put walkways and paths. They'll both delineate space and provide visual interest.

How much privacy do you want—or need? Perhaps you'd like both public and private areas. If, for example, the garden will be used for entertaining or needs to include a place for family meals, you'll want at least that part secluded from view.

This is the time to evaluate your need for turf. Do you want a soft, resilient surface for children to play on or perhaps as a cooling surface beside a swimming pool? Perhaps you entertain

Before landscape redesign, water flowed down hillside into gully and under house. Now, dry creek carries off seasonal runoff and also functions as a decorative rock garden. Landscape architect: Nancy Hardesty.

If You're Not Ready to Start Over

An old landscape can easily be renovated in stages to make it less thirsty. That way you'll spread the work and the expense over several years, and you'll avoid disrupting the entire garden at once. If you have an in-ground irrigation system already, it can usually be adjusted to water your new plantings less frequently.

Assessing what's there. Before making any changes, take a good look at what you already have. What features of your garden could work better in function or design? What weaknesses are there, such as dry or wet spots in the water system, and tired or old plants?

Take a careful look at your existing plants. Identify which are low-water consumers. You may already have a number of them, but you may be watering them as if they were heavy users; or they may be planted among thirsty ones.

Isolate the features and plants you want to keep and work a new design around them.

Zoning your garden. First, sketch on paper the existing zones; next, mark any rearrangement you wish to make. You can then gradually uproot, transplant, or regroup to get your plants of like water needs together.

Targeting areas for improvement. Depending on the extent of the changes you want to make in your garden, you may need to devise a long-range plan. Try to put your money and time where you'll see the water-saving results first. One way to do this is to remove the few thirsty plants from an otherwise water-thrifty bed. Or this might be the year you reduce or eliminate your lawn and put in ground cover. Next year, perhaps, you'll add a deck.

Checking maintenance and watering practices. A few simple changes that involve little work or money but that usually result in substantial water savings can be made at the outset. Here are some practical suggestions:

■ ***Mulch.*** Your flower and vegetable beds especially will benefit from mulch. It seals in moisture, discourages weeds, and acts as an insulator. A long-term benefit of many mulches will be soil improvement.

■ ***Weed.*** Pull up or hoe moisture-stealing weeds as soon as they make an appearance.

■ ***Water carefully.*** By getting a good water-management program in place for your existing garden or repairing an old, inefficient system, you can often realize an immediate reduction in water consumption.

■ ***Take care of turf.*** If you dethatch and aerate your lawn, water can seep into root zones more easily, promoting healthy, deep roots.

Providing year-round beauty in an arid climate are pink-flowering lemon thyme (Thymus citriodorus) and yellow-flowering goldmoss sedum (Sedum acre). Three varieties of penstemon add their brilliance to this high-desert garden. Landscape designer: Ben Haggard of The Well-Tempered Garden.

frequently and want a spillover area off your deck or patio where friends can congregate. With careful planning, you may find that even a lawn that takes up only a fraction of a garden's overall space can still offer enough room for playing and entertaining, as well as that welcome sight of cool green grass.

Often, a small lawn with a definite shape becomes a special place. A small semicircular lawn, for instance, seems like a private glen when enveloped by trees, shrubs, and rocks.

If your garden's function is likely to change in the future, try to plan for alternative uses from the start. A play area for children can be adapted for other pastimes when the children have outgrown their need for it.

Seasonal needs. Ask yourself how your use of the garden will change throughout the year. If you live where temperature extremes keep you indoors part of the year or you're regularly away from home during certain months, such seasonal changes will affect your design and choice of plants. You may, for example, want to include some plants for year-round greenery if most of the garden is dormant in winter. Or maybe you'll want plenty of spring flowering plants if that's when you use the garden the most.

Maintenance goals. A waterwise garden is a low-maintenance garden because it's designed to flourish with lots of help from nature and not much assistance from you. Even so, your garden will need some care— mulching, weeding, pest and disease control, and occasional pruning, as well as some watering and frequent adjustments of irrigation controllers. (Good maintenance practices for waterwise gardens are discussed on pages 49–53.)

If you have little time for yard work, your goal will be to streamline your maintenance chores as much as possible. One way to do this is to make extensive use of decks, paving, and low-care ground covers.

On the other hand, if gardening is one of your hobbies, you'll want to focus on your special interest, whether it be growing roses, vegetables, or cut

Hot spot in bot climate is congenial home to an assortment of water-thrifty plants. Colorful accents are purple Mexican bush sage (Salvia leucantha), gray-leafed dusty miller (Centaurea cineraria) with yellow flowers, and pink-blossomed Mexican evening primrose (Oenothera berlandieri). Landscape architects: Erik Katzmaier and Yana Ruzicka.

flowers. In that case, consider setting aside the greatest portion of the landscape for very low water use so you'll have enough water for your pet plants.

Such a special interest is likely to influence your garden design. For example, the one hot, sunny area of your property may have to be devoted to your prize tomatoes. As you plan, though, be sure the needs of your hobby don't interfere with your overall waterwise goals.

Studying Your Site

A careful assessment of your property is vital to the development of your design plan. Your garden's microclimate and other special characteristics will, in large part, determine your choice of plants and their location in your yard.

Climate. To be waterwise, a garden must be respectful of local climate conditions: temperature, annual rainfall patterns, winds, seasonal humidity, and cloud or fog cover. Every waterwise garden relies on plants that live comfortably in the local climate, plants that are either native to your area or from similar climates.

Microclimates. Most gardens encompass several microclimates—areas defined by the amount of sun, heat, and moisture they receive. A tree, for example, often creates a microclimate around it. The cool, shady space beneath it provides very different growing conditions from, say, an area exposed to the reflected sunlight of a south-facing wall.

By adjusting conditions on your

property—adding a sun screen or a windbreak, for example—you can broaden your choice of plants. As always, though, keep water requirements in mind: you'll want to avoid plants that need more than a slight adjustment of the environment.

Paying attention to the microclimates on your property helps you locate zones and choose appropriate plants for them.

Exposure. Sun and shade patterns in each area of your garden will also be important for identifying the zones. Knowing the patterns will help you determine where to locate a patio or barbecue, or where to plant low-water-use plants. Note the path of the sun in your yard and how its shadow patterns change from December 21 (when the sun is lowest in the southern sky) to June 21 (when it's highest).

As a rule, south and west exposures result in the greatest water loss, especially near buildings and paved surfaces. You can save water in those locations by putting your least thirsty plants there. In areas exposed to intense sun, use hardscape judiciously; it can easily heat up in the sun.

North and east sides of homes tend to be cooler and wetter. If you live in a hot-weather region, that's where you may want to plant your thirstier plants or build your deck or patio.

By keeping exposure to sun in mind, you can use plants that both make the design work best and help you conserve water. For example, a deciduous tree (one that loses its leaves in the winter) should probably be planted on the south side. There it can provide summer shade, yet allow the sun to warm the house in winter.

Wind. Wind patterns are less predictable than sun and shade, but no less a factor in planning your garden design. Generally, whatever you do to moderate wind will result in water savings.

Note wind directions and windy times of year. If you're new to the area, ask neighbors about typical wind character. Look at mature trees and windbreaks to see whether they lean, indicating wind direction and intensity.

Coyote brush (Baccharis pulularis) thrives in a wide range of soils and climates, from sandy soil and coastal fog to heavy alkaline soil and desert heat.

Soil conditions. Many plants have very specific soil requirements. Each soil type retains water differently and provides different growing conditions.

If you're unsure about the condition of your soil, have it tested by your County Cooperative Extension Office, a commercial soil-testing lab, or a nursery. A soils report can tell you how much organic material to add to your soil to increase its ability to absorb and hold water. (For more information on the different types of soil and how to make adjustments, see the chapter that begins on page 29.)

Drainage. Good drainage, related to soil types, is important for growing healthy plants and managing irrigation. You'll want to make sure that water drains properly so that no standing puddles are formed. To improve drainage, see the discussion of causes and remedies on page 33.

Hillsides. Steep slopes with south and west exposures waste water through rapid evaporation. An unthirsty ground cover can slow water loss, as can shade trees and mulching. For a listing of plants suitable for hillsides, turn to page 60.

Legal considerations. Before proceeding very far in the planning stages, be sure to learn what, if any, legal restrictions apply to construction or landscaping on your property. Check city or county ordinances for any limitations regarding fence heights or setbacks. Permits may be required for new structures or in-ground watering systems.

Designing Your Garden

Now's the time to get out your graph and tracing paper and begin to experiment with garden designs, taking into consideration the main principles of waterwise gardening—zoning the landscape by grouping plants of like needs and limiting the amount of turf you in-

Retaining walls planted with unthirsty woolly thyme (Thymus pseudolanuginosus) cascade down this hillside garden. Small, inviting lawn provides play space and lounging area. Landscape architect: John Herbst, Jr.

A Sample Site Analysis

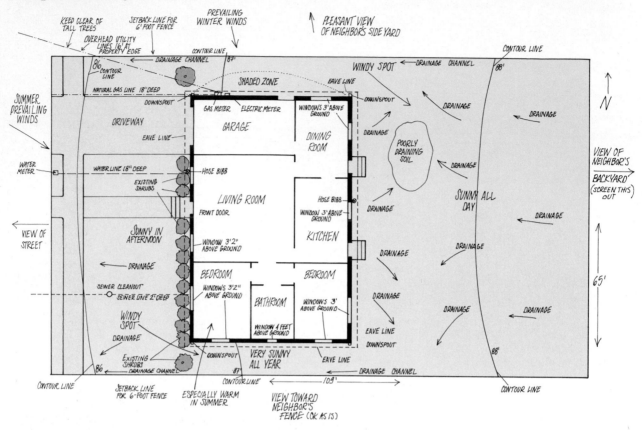

Map shows all important features and characteristics of property, including location and orientation of structures, sun and wind patterns, views, and slope and drainage. Drawing becomes foundation on which final landscape plan is built.

clude. Aim to design a landscape that's not only water-thrifty but also pleasing to you and in keeping with your home's appearance.

A waterwise garden can be any style, as long as it can tolerate—even thrive on—the temperature extremes, rainfall, and soil conditions of your property. When the landscape fits those limits, you're working with nature and making the most of your area's resources.

Mapping Your Property

The first step in turning your ideas into reality is to develop a base map. Ideally, you'll have an old construction plan that identifies property lines and locates the house. (It's best to verify measurements.) If not, you'll need to draw up a base plan yourself.

Developing a base map. Using graph paper so objects will be in scale (typically ¼ or ⅛ inch to 1 foot), precisely position the house, property line, walks, patios, trees, fences, and any other structures or distinctive features on your map. Check with your utility company to find out if any utility lines are buried underground on your property and mark them on your drawing. Note also where you'll tap into your house's water supply.

Creating a site analysis. With tracing paper taped over your base map, make a site analysis, using a bold pen to indicate positive and negative factors that play major roles in the existing landscape. Highlight everything that could affect privacy, views, outdoor activities, and plant growth.

Mark, for example, views that need screening, the direction of summer and winter winds (to identify windbreak needs), sunny and shady areas, overhanging trees, slopes, and areas that should stay open for walkways, as well as any storage or work spaces.

Drawing a plan. Tape a piece of tracing paper over the base map, keeping the site analysis nearby for reference, and sketch in the elements you want. Take into consideration all the needs you determined earlier—such as a built-in barbecue, a play area, a shade arbor—and draw in areas for each of them.

Looking at your site analysis, you'll see which areas are exposed to full sun in the summer, which to wind, and so on. All are factors that help identify low-, moderate-, and high-water-use zones. You'll probably want to sketch several alternative plans before settling on the best one. Once you've decided on a design, draw up the final plan accurately and to scale.

Choosing Landscape Elements

The next step is the one most gardeners especially enjoy—identifying specific plants and hardscape materials to use in the garden.

Selecting plants. The key to a successful waterwise garden is choosing the right plants. But remember that unthirsty trees, shrubs, vines, ground covers, and perennials alone don't save water. They must be planted in the right place, in soil that drains well, and where they'll receive the right amount of sun or shade. Then they need to be watered and maintained appropriately. Be sure to group plants with the same water needs.

Desert garden has two planting zones. In narrow bed in foreground, tobira (Pittosporum tobira) and cycad grow in shade of olive tree. Beyond paved patio are less thirsty plants—Texas ranger (Leucophyllum frutescens) and rosemary. Design: Doug Terpstra.

Three-zone garden groups plants by water needs. Trellised grapevine and small lawn keep mini-oasis cool and inviting in summer. Desert marigolds (Baileya multiradiata) provide color in desert zone in winter and spring. Design: Warren Jones.

Being a waterwise gardener doesn't mean you can't have some plants in your landscape that aren't suited to your site and climate. But those plants should be held to a minimum and placed where you can see them best and easily provide the extra care they demand. Perhaps you'll have them in a few containers on the deck or in a planting bed beside the entryway of your house. The major part of your garden then will be given to well-adapted—and still beautiful—plants that thrive with less struggle and care.

When selecting plants, remember that it will take time for them to fill out and mature. Instead of overplanting at first and then having to remove crowded plants, see if you can tolerate a bit of sparseness at the beginning (for planting help, see page 32). You'll end up with a stronger and healthier waterwise garden in the long run.

For detailed information about the appearance and growth habits of a wide range of unthirsty plants, turn to the chapter beginning on page 65.

Ground covers combine invitingly with stone and poured-in-place concrete paving. Filling in pockets are blue fescue (Festuca ovina glauca), Pacific Coast iris, lamb's ears (Stachys byzantina), succulents, and more.

Hardscape variety contributes to landscape interest. Weathered brick pavement serves as patio floor; river-washed stones provide a footpath into garden. Landscape architects: Erik Katzmaier and Yana Ruzicka.

Gray blue stones lie in a streamlike path in a bed of tan gravel chips. In front is dwarf pomegranate (Punica granatum 'Nana'); aloe grows in pot behind. Landscape architect: Isabelle Greene.

Designing decks, walkways, and other hardscape elements. The structural features of a waterwise garden take on extra importance because they're often prominent in the landscape. Selecting materials that harmonize with the appearance of your house and with each other makes design unity easier to achieve.

Many hardscape materials can heat up uncomfortably when exposed to the sun, increasing evaporation, so take care where you place them. You may not, for instance, want stone surfaces next to your house on a south or west exposure.

Well-stocked nurseries and building supply outlets offer a wide range of materials for hardscape, including wood, brick, stone, concrete and other pavers, tile, crushed rock, bark, gravel, and even crushed sea shells. The materials you select will depend on how and where you'll use them.

■ *Wood* is generally an excellent material for decking and some walkways. Railroad ties make sturdy pathways, steps, planters, and retaining walls. Wood rounds can be laid in a sand bed and used as stepping-stones; you can surround them with gravel, bark, sand, or soil.

Be sure to use only decay-resistant redwood, cypress, or cedar heartwood, or pressure-treated lumber.

■ *Brick* often works well for walkways, fences, steps, mowing strips, and borders around planting beds. If you set the bricks in a bed of sand instead of mortar, water will be able to penetrate the ground beneath.

■ *Stone* comes in a range of colors and sizes and fits a number of garden uses. It often makes an excellent paving or mulching surface. Among the many pleasing choices are fieldstone, flagstone, slate, cobblestones, and river rocks.

For durability and rustic appeal, fieldstone is hard to beat. Although the stones are heavy and sometimes awkward to handle, with just a shovel and a little muscle you can create a path of stepping-stones that looks like a natural element in the landscape.

■ *Concrete pavers and poured concrete* are versatile and durable. Pavers are an inexpensive alternative to brick and have the advantage of allowing water to seep through. Poured concrete can be formed to any shape and even stamped with special patterning tools to give the finished surface a range of appearances. The disadvantage of poured concrete is that it's not porous.

If you do select concrete (and it's often the best choice for such areas as driveways), you might want to slope it, put in drainpipes, or otherwise try to capture and direct rainfall.

Planning a watering system. Watering systems are best designed last—after all the zones, hardscape, and plantings

Spreading olive tree in background anchors Mediterranean-style garden in dry-summer region. Fountain grass (Pennisetum setaceum) grows in small bed at corner of pool. Stone paving separates pool from gray-foliaged plants, including artemisia and santolina. Landscape architect: Jack Chandler.

have been decided upon. An efficient watering system, whether it's a drip system, an underground one, or simply a garden hose and sprinklers, should meet the needs of each planted area. Try to make the system as flexible as possible, with multiple control stations, so you can easily water each zone according to its need.

For a detailed discussion of the various watering methods, turn to the chapter that begins on page 35.

Finding Professional Help

A variety of landscape specialists have expertise in remodeling existing gardens or designing new ones. How much professional help you'll want or need depends on what design and installation work you want to do yourself.

When you're looking for a professional, it's always a good idea to ask for referrals from friends and neighbors. Once you find someone you're interested in, check references by asking for a list of previous clients so you can see examples and talk with the owners.

Be sure to find out whether the professional is interested in waterwise gardening and knowledgeable about plants. For help in finding someone in your area, call or write the National Xeriscape Council, Inc., 940 E. Fifty-first St., Austin, TX 78751-2241, phone (512) 454-8626.

You may want to do much of the design and installation work yourself, turning to specialists for such tasks as installing a watering system or building a masonry wall or walkway. The most common sources of help are landscape architects, landscape designers, landscape contractors, and nursery personnel. Knowing what each of these professionals does can help you pick the right one for your job.

Landscape architects generally hold a degree in landscape architecture from an accredited university. In many states they're licensed, on the basis of work experience, education, and test results, to create landscape plans for a fee. They can provide a range of services from hourly consultation to preparing complete design and construction drawings.

Deck-edge garden blends gray- and green-leafed yellow-flowering santolinas, purplish Mexican bush sage (Salvia leucantha), and rosemary. Design: Rudolph's Landscape Service.

Landscape designers are less easily defined as they're not licensed or certified. Their training and experience can vary widely. Many are graduates of horticultural or garden design programs. Others have some training as landscape architects. In some states, they're barred from certain kinds of structural designing.

Landscape contractors are trained and, in most states, licensed to install paving, planting, structures, lighting, and irrigation systems. They implement the plans of landscape architects and designers; many will also design the projects they build.

Nursery personnel are often available for garden consultation. In some states, certification through the state association tells you that they have passed tests on such topics as plants, diseases, insects, weeds, and soils. They're also likely to be familiar with local growing conditions and with the plants that do well in your area.

Some nurseries have a designer on staff who provides plans for fountains and other features if you buy the materials from the nursery. Others have a separate landscape division that will provide complete design and construction services for a fee.

Working with Soil

The path to water wisdom begins with an understanding of your soil. Not merely an anchor for plant roots, soil also serves as a reservoir for water and nutrients.

Water absorption and retention are influenced by the composition of your soil. In turn, they govern the amount of water you should apply and the frequency of application.

Soil Characteristics & Types

Despite its plain appearance, garden soil is a complex mixture of mineral particles, organic matter, microorganisms, water, and air.

The characteristics of the mineral particles—their sizes and shapes—determine their classifications, ranging from clay (the smallest) to sand (the largest). Soil types are also graded by dominant particle type.

The smallest and largest soil particle types—clay and sand—give their names to two kinds of soil. A third variety, called loam, combines clay and sand particles with intermediate-size particles called silt. The characteristics of all three are described on page 30.

Many garden soils contain a mixture of soil particles. Still, it's important to determine which type your soil most closely resembles. Then you can use this knowledge, along with information on water absorption, to determine the most effective watering practices in your garden.

Adding organic matter improves aeration and water penetration. Soil air is vital to good root growth and to the health of soil microorganisms.

Amending the soil improves its texture, allowing better water and root penetration. Best time to add organic amendments is when you can work the entire garden, digging or tilling them into the soil to 8 to 10 inches.

Clay soils contain very small, flattened particles that pack closely together, leaving little space between particles for soil, air, and water. This "heavy," or "adobe," soil is sticky when wet and cracks when dry. To test for a clay or claylike soil, pick up a handful of wet soil and shape it into a ball. Clay will feel slippery; when you let it go, it won't crumble (see photo below), and if you squeeze it, the excess will ooze through your fingers in ribbons.

Dense clay soils absorb water slowly and retain it well; plants growing in clay soil can go longer without watering than those in other soil types. Drainage—the downward movement of water—is slow, which means that the loss of soluble nutrients by leaching is also slow, one reason many clay soils are quite fertile. (For a discussion of drainage, see "Soil Problems & Remedies" on page 33.)

Sandy soils are the opposite of clay; particles are larger (up to 250 times the size of clay particles) and rounded rather than flattened, allowing for larger pore spaces between particles than clay soils have. Sandy soil feels gritty rather than sticky or slimy; when you squeeze a handful of wet sandy soil, it will fall apart when you release your grip or give it a slight prod.

Soil Particles & Types

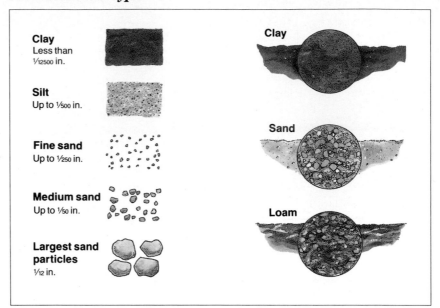

Clay
Less than ¹⁄₁₂₅₀₀ in.

Silt
Up to ¹⁄₅₀₀ in.

Fine sand
Up to ¹⁄₂₅₀ in.

Medium sand
Up to ¹⁄₅₀ in.

Largest sand particles
¹⁄₁₂ in.

Clay

Sand

Loam

Moist clay soil, formed into a smooth ball, doesn't crumble when you let it go.

Water enters sandy soil easily and percolates through it rapidly, taking the dissolved nutrients along with it. Sandy soil is therefore well drained but poor in nutrients. Plants growing in it need more frequent watering and fertilizing than plants in other soil types.

Loam is a gardener's term for soil intermediate between sand and clay. Loam contains a mixture of clay, sand, and silt particles and organic matter. Considered the ideal gardening soil, loam drains well (but doesn't dry too fast), while nutrients leach through at a moderate rate. These soils also contain sufficient air for healthy root growth.

To the touch, loam feels less gritty than sand, less sticky than clay. If you squeeze a handful, it will form a pliable ball that breaks apart with a gentle prod.

Organic Matter: A Vital Component

Essential to the quality and fertility of all soils—and particularly needed in clay and sandy soils—is organic matter, the decaying remains of once-living plants and animals. In nature, these materials fall to the earth, where they then decompose, aided by microorganisms in the soil. Gardeners can accelerate this slow process by digging organic amendments into the soil before planting.

Even the best of soils can benefit from the application of an organic amendment, which improves aeration and water penetration.

In clay soils, the decaying matter wedges between soil particles and groups of particles, opening up the earth so that water, air, and roots can penetrate more easily. Runoff and puddling—two common watering problems in clay soil—are reduced when organic matter is added.

In sandy soils, organic matter lodges in the relatively large spaces between particles, slowing the percolation of water through the soil so that moisture and dissolved nutrients are retained longer.

Types of Organic Amendments

Organic materials—such as nitrogen-stabilized wood by-products (shredded bark or aged sawdust), peat moss, animal manures, and commercially prepared composts—are sold in nurseries and garden centers, usually in 2-cubic-foot bags. Some materials—primarily wood products and various agricultural by-products—may also be purchased in bulk, generally by the cubic yard, from nonnursery suppliers; for sources, look in the Yellow Pages under "Soil Conditioners" and "Landscape Equipment and Supplies."

Most commercially packaged wood-product soil amendments either contain enough nitrogen to satisfy the soil organisms or have been nitrogen fortified. But if you're using raw wood shavings or a similar noncomposted, low-nitrogen product, you'll probably need to add nitrogen to the soil, as described below.

Adding Organic Amendments

When you add organic amendments to your soil, be generous and mix them in deeply and uniformly. The mixing will add some air to the soil, and the amendments will help keep it there.

Eventually, organic matter will be completely reduced by the soil microorganisms, and new material should be added. With frequently renewed beds, such as for vegetables and annuals, add organic amendments each time you prepare the soil. In permanent plantings, an organic mulch will provide material for continued decomposition so the topsoil will remain permeable.

If you plan to use raw (noncomposted) materials—particularly sawdust or wood shavings—remember that the soil organisms that break down organic materials need nitrogen to thrive and multiply. If they cannot get all the nitrogen they require from the organic material itself, they'll draw upon any available nitrogen in the soil, stealing the nitrogen vital for root growth. The result can be a temporary nitrogen depletion and reduced plant growth.

To add nitrogen to the soil, scatter ammonium sulfate over the noncomposted material before tilling; use 1 pound of ammonium sulfate for each 1-inch-deep layer of noncomposted organic matter spread over 100 square feet. Mix the amendments thoroughly into the soil before planting. A year later, apply half the initial amount of ammonium sulfate over the area, and in the third and fourth years, use a quarter as much.

Preparing the Soil

Garden planting may be categorized as either total area planting or installation of individual plants. How you prepare your soil depends on which approach you plan to take.

Total Area Planting

When you are planting a new garden or totally remodeling a large area, the best approach is to clear the ground of weeds and unwanted plants, and then thoroughly dig or till the area to be planted. At the same time, you'll want to improve the soil with organic amendments and perhaps incorporate certain nutrients, as described below.

The easiest preparation is to lightly till the area, spread the organic matter over the soil, and then thoroughly dig or till it through the depth of the prepared soil. Add a volume of organic matter equal to a fourth to a third of the soil volume—for example, dig a 2-inch layer of organic matter into 8 to 10 inches of soil. (To calculate the amount needed, figure that a 2-cubic-foot bag of organic material will convert to a layer about 3 inches deep over 8 square feet of soil. If you are using bulk materials, plan for 1 cubic yard to provide a 3-inch layer over 108 square feet.)

At the same time that you add organic amendments to the soil, you can also add fertilizers. Of the three main nutrients—nitrogen, phosphorus, and potassium—only nitrogen is water-soluble; it can be applied at any time by scattering on the soil surface.

For all practical purposes, phosphorus and potassium are insoluble; in order to be of any value, they must be mixed into the soil that roots will inhabit. To add phosphorus and potassium to your soil, scatter the amount of fertilizer recommended on the package (usually given in pounds per square feet) over the soil, then till it in along with the organic amendments.

At this time you can also add any materials recommended to alter your soil's acidity or alkalinity (as explained in "Soil Problems & Remedies," page 33).

Soils' Water-holding Capacity

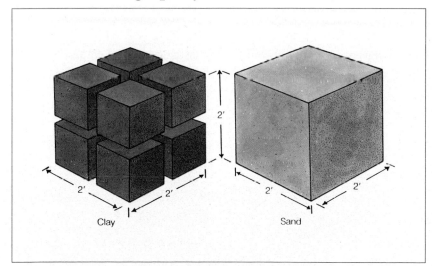

Clay

Sand

To understand the difference in water-holding capacity between clay and sandy soils, visualize the 2-foot cube as one sand particle and the eight 1-foot cubes as smaller clay particles. The 2-foot cube has the same outside dimensions as the eight 1-foot cubes placed together. But the cubes representing clay particles have a total of 48 square feet of surface to which water can adhere, while the large cube representing sand has only 24 square feet of surface.

Individual Installation

When individual shrubs and trees are set out in an existing garden, there's no opportunity to amend a large area of soil. Under these conditions, your soil type determines the planting method.

If your soil is sandy to sandy loam, add organic matter to the soil you'll be returning to the planting hole. Use one part amendment to two parts garden soil. The organic matter will help get the plants off to a good start.

In heavier soils, however, organically amended backfill soil absorbs water at a faster rate than the surrounding garden soil can absorb it. In effect, the planting hole can become a subterranean basin in which roots will die from saturation that restricts vital soil air. When planting a tree or shrub in heavy soil, return the soil unamended to the planting hole. Use an organic mulch around the plant; this will gradually improve the top layer of soil.

Planting Guidelines

When you set out plants in your garden, it's important to pay close attention to their water needs until the plants become established. Even so, you can reduce the amount of water needed if you heed the following guidelines.

Best Size to Plant

You might think that large plants set out into the garden will reach mature size more quickly than small plants. In reality, the smaller plant (with its smaller root system) establishes more rapidly when planted; often, its growth will outstrip a larger plant of the same kind planted concurrently.

The larger plant has a larger root system, which takes longer to adapt to its new environment. During this adjustment period, a large plant may grow at a relatively slow rate.

When first set out, a plant needs more frequent watering than it will once it is established. Also, a larger plant demands more water than a smaller one.

Unless you need a large specimen plant for immediate effect, shop for smaller but healthy individuals. For woody plants—trees, shrubs, vines—choose the 1-gallon size rather than the 5-gallon or larger; when buying perennials, select plants in 4- and 6-inch pots instead of those available in 1-gallon containers.

Best Times to Plant

The best time of year to plant trees, shrubs, vines, and many perennials varies by region; you should plant them when they will have the longest possible time to become established before temperature or weather extremes put the plants under stress. Planting times are more precise for annuals and vegetables; most are either warm- or cool-season plants.

Fall and winter are the best planting seasons in mild-winter regions; roots grow during the cool part of the year, so plants will be ready for more vigorous growth when warm weather arrives.

If you live in a cold-weather region, where soil routinely freezes and snow can be expected, plant in early spring just after the soil can be worked.

Gardeners who live in low- and intermediate-elevation deserts should set out plants just as soon as cool weather arrives.

Unless you live in a cool-summer area, summer is the least desirable time to plant. Hot weather puts extra stress on newly set out plants, and they are slower to establish. During that time, you'll need to pay close attention to watering so plants won't wilt, perhaps watering both morning and evening.

Organic Amendments

Organic amendments, tilled into the soil before planting, are used to improve soil composition, aeration, and water penetration. Among packaged choices are commercial compost (left), which typically consists of sludge mixed with wood by-products. Sawdust (right) is fortified with nitrogen so that decomposing organisms will have ample nitrogen and won't have to draw upon soil nitrogen needed for plant roots.

Soil Problems & Remedies

Sometimes, poor plant performance is due to a soil problem. Below are several common soil conditions and ways to correct or minimize them.

Drainage

The most frequent physical soil problem is poor drainage—where water moves very slowly into the soil. Correction or careful management is necessary if you want to grow a broad variety of plants. Here are some of the causes of, and remedies for, poor drainage.

Deep clay soils. Drainage is usually slow in deep clay soils. To improve water penetration and reduce runoff, mix liberal amounts of organic matter into the soil. Set out plants on mounds raised a few inches above the soil grade and then mulch liberally between the plants.

Those plants that are especially sensitive to poor drainage will grow best in raised beds filled with porous soil (or native soil heavily amended with organic matter).

You can improve drainage in some clay soils if you scatter gypsum or lime over the soil surface and dig or till it into the soil. Either amendment causes the tiny clay particles to group together into larger units, called crumbs; this creates a looser soil structure with improved aeration and drainage.

Use gypsum (calcium sulfate) in the high-sodium, "black alkali" soils of the Southwest and West. In acid-soil regions (generally where rainfall is plentiful), lime will improve soil structure while also raising soil pH (see "Acidity & Alkalinity," at right). Before using either material, check with your County Cooperative Extension Office for advisability and guidelines.

Water management is a key to success in deep clay soils. Don't overwater; let the top 2 to 3 inches of soil dry out between waterings.

Compacted soil. At new homesites, heavy construction equipment can seriously compact soil, leaving it difficult to dig, poorly drained, and virtually impossible for plant roots to penetrate. Special soil-loosening equipment—capable of ripping the soil to a depth of 18 inches or so—may remedy the problem. This is a job best left to a landscape contractor or other professional.

Hardpan. A tight, impervious layer of soil, called hardpan, can cause problems if it lies near the surface. Even if the surface soil is permeable, a hardpan layer beneath it will prevent good drainage, causing problems similar to those created by deep clay and compacted soils.

If the hardpan layer is fairly thin, you may be able to dig planting holes through it into more porous subsoil below; holes should be at least 1 foot in diameter. If a hardpan layer is too thick to dig through, your best solution is to plant in raised beds filled with good, porous soil.

Acidity & Alkalinity

Although invisible to the gardener's eye, the acidity or alkalinity of a soil also affects plant performance. This soil condition is expressed in pH numbers on a scale of 1 to 14. With a neutral midpoint of pH 7, the scale ranks acid soils at pH 6.9 and below, and alkaline (or "basic") soils at pH 7.1 and above.

Moderate readings in either direction will suit a broad range of plants, but highly acid or alkaline soils will hinder growth of all but a few plants. It's always a good idea to choose kinds known to perform well in your soil's pH (acid-preferring plants in acid soil, for example).

A soil test will tell you the acidity or alkalinity of your soil. You can have the test run by a professional laboratory; or you can do it yourself, with slightly less precise results, using a soil test kit (look for test kits at nurseries and garden centers). If the test indicates the need to raise or lower the pH of your soil, check with your County Cooperative Extension Office for the best way to proceed.

Acid soil. Most common in regions where rainfall is plentiful, acidity is often associated with sandy soils and soils high in organic matter. The addition of lime will raise the pH of an acid soil. Be sure that any fertilizers you use don't have an acid reaction.

Alkaline soil. Common in regions where rainfall is light, alkaline soil is high in calcium carbonate (lime) or certain other minerals, such as sodium. Many plants will grow well in moderately alkaline soil; others won't thrive because the alkalinity reduces the availability of elements necessary for their growth. Chlorosis, usually caused by an iron deficiency, is one common example.

To reduce high alkalinity, liberally add organic amendments, such as peat moss, ground bark, or sawdust (see page 31); or fertilize with an acid-type fertilizer. For soils with a very high pH, use soil sulfur.

Watering Guidelines & Methods

Wise watering ensures that plants always receive enough water to thrive. Equally important is a second goal: to eliminate water wastage that can occur when plants are overwatered and water is squandered in runoff or evaporation.

The amount of water your plant needs depends on two factors: the depth and spread of its root system, and the amount of water needed in your soil to moisten the plant's root zone. In general, plants growing in sandy soil need less water at a time but at more frequent intervals than the same plants growing in heavier soils.

The frequency of watering depends on the rate of water use by plants. This depends on the plant's inherent water need, but it also is influenced by season and weather. Light intensity, temperature, humidity, and wind affect a plant's transpiration rate. This is why summer —with the year's maximum amount of daylight, highest temperatures, and (in some regions) the lowest humidities —calls for the greatest attention to garden watering.

Competition from nearby plants also plays a part. The more roots that occupy a given volume of soil, the more quickly will water in that soil be used. This is the primary reason for removing weeds from the garden.

Simple Water Economy

Wise garden watering emphasizes economy without deprivation. To achieve economy, you should conserve water use, reduce your garden's need for it, and install an efficient watering system.

Ways to Conserve Water

Consider first the various ways to make the most of available water. Following are some suggestions for minimizing water waste.

Newly planted junipers will receive their water by drip irrigation. Here, existing rigid-pipe sprinkler system is being retrofitted to accommodate flexible drip tubing.

■ **Water early in the day.** To minimize water loss from evaporation, water in the early hours. Sun is less intense, and winds are likely to be absent or light.

■ **Water deeply and thoroughly.** Most plants (except for naturally shallow-rooted kinds) develop roots throughout the soil depth at which water, air, and nutrients are present. Light watering encourages shallow rooting, and shallow-rooted plants need frequent watering (soil dries from the surface downward). Deep and thorough watering should be practiced—but as infrequently as your soil allows.

■ **Eliminate runoff.** Don't waste water by irrigating paved surfaces. If your sprinkler system showers water over sidewalks, patios, or driveways, change the sprinkler heads or the system design.

Sloping land and heavy, claylike soils invite runoff—the first due to gravity, the second because of slow water penetration. To solve a runoff problem, you need to adjust the rate at which water is applied.

With sprinklers, you can improve penetration by watering for several successive short intervals, leaving time between them for water to soak in. You also should use low-precipitation-rate sprinkler heads, mentioned below and described on page 40. A drip-irrigation system (see pages 43–46) lets you select from a variety of low-volume emitters.

■ **Use low-volume watering devices.** If you already have an underground sprinkler system, you can upgrade it by installing water-conservative sprinkler heads. The low-precipitation-rate heads can eliminate runoff waste. Use matched-precipitation-rate heads to equalize water distribution over an area. For more information, see page 40.

The ultimate low-volume applicators are found among the drip-irrigation emitters and heads, which are described on pages 43–44.

■ **Change water schedules seasonally.** Water demand varies by the season, with greatest need during the summer. Adjust your watering routine so that you water less frequently during the cooler months of the year.

■ **Automate your watering.** Time is the greatest water waster—leaving the water running longer than it is needed. Runoff is the most conspicuous evidence, but you also can waste water by soaking the soil too thoroughly at one time. An automatic electronic controller can operate simple or complex watering schedules, so that plants are watered precisely when and for the length of time you want. See page 41 for more information.

Reducing Your Water Needs

If you are developing a new garden, you can reduce your water needs through careful planning, as described on pages 11–27. But even an established garden can benefit from some of the following suggestions.

■ **Choose drought-tolerant plants.** Drought tolerant is a relative term—the degree of dryness depending on the climate. The key is to look for plants that need little or no supplemental water *under your conditions.*

■ **Group plants with similar water needs.** Don't mix plants that need little or no watering with those that need regular watering; this wastes water on the unthirsty plants and can even hamper (or terminate) their performance. If you group plants that need regular watering, you can put them on a separate watering system and schedule.

■ **Eliminate weeds.** These garden intruders consume water needed by your more desirable plants.

■ **Mulch to retard evaporation.** If you spread an organic mulch several inches deep over the soil, it acts as an insulating blanket. It helps retard evaporation from the soil surface and keeps the surface cooler than bare soil. For more information, see page 49.

■ **Reconsider the lawn.** Of all the usual garden features, the lawn consumes the most water per square foot of garden area. If a lawn is an essential part of your garden, consider ways to diminish its thirst. First, reduce its size to the smallest that will satisfy you; less lawn needs less water. Second, choose a grass or grass blend adapted to your climate, as described on page 63.

For a common-sense approach to water-thrifty lawn care, see page 47.

■ **Use soil polymers.** These gel-like particles absorb and hold water and dissolved nutrients. They help retain moisture for container plants (see facing page) and may be useful in large beds.

Water Delivery Systems

Some water is essential to the growth of any plant, even one that's drought tolerant.

For home gardens, there are two main methods of watering. One is a stationary water system: an underground sprinkler system using rigid pipes and fixed-position watering heads, or a drip-irrigation system, which features flexible plastic tubing laid on or just beneath the soil surface.

The other method is a simple portable system, using a sprinkler head attached to the end of a hose; you place the sprinkler every time you water.

Hoses & Sprinklers

If you water with one or more hose-end sprinklers, you can choose from a varied array with differing modes of dispersing water. Use these sprinklers in small gardens where one or two placements will cover the entire area to be watered. In a larger garden, moving the sprinkler becomes a nuisance. You also must overlap the coverage so all plants will get adequate water.

You'll waste some water with any hose-end sprinkler, though the extent of waste varies. Spray thrown into the air is subject to evaporation and wind drift; the quantity of water delivered may be more than the soil can absorb easily—especially in claylike soils—resulting in puddling and runoff after a short period of watering. And if the sprinkler isn't positioned carefully, it's easy to water paved surfaces along with your plants.

Choosing a Sprinkler

If you have heavy, slow-draining soil, you should choose a sprinkler that dis-

Watering Plants in Containers

Plants growing in containers need more water than similar ones growing in the ground due to their limited root systems and exposure to heat and wind. Regular watering is especially necessary during extended hot or dry periods, when plants are under extra stress. Even under normal circumstances, watering can be time consuming, especially if you dutifully tend each container with a hose or watering can.

It's not necessary to sacrifice the pleasures of container plants in your water-thrifty garden. Discussed below are several ways you can save both water and watering time and still have healthy plants.

Reducing Water Use

For container gardens, one key to conserving water is to lengthen the intervals between needed waterings.

Use large containers. Initially, the larger the volume of soil, the slower it dries. Therefore, large pots—10 inches in diameter and larger—will need watering less often. As plants grow, filling the soil with roots, the watering intervals will shorten.

Use nonporous containers. Unglazed clay pots are porous, allowing moisture to transpire through their sides. Wooden pots and barrels and concrete containers are also porous, but to a lesser extent. The most efficient pots for retaining moisture are those made of glazed pottery or plastic, materials that allow little moisture loss; soil in these pots will remain moist longer than soil in porous containers of comparable size.

You can reduce or eliminate the porosity of a container if you paint the inside with asphalt roofing sealer. Brush-on liquids are easiest to spread; gels are much easier to find and can be brushed on when warm, but they're messier to use and take longer to apply. To keep an attractive appearance in clay and concrete containers, you can leave unsealed the portion that will show above the soil line. In wooden containers, paint the sealer all the way to the rim; otherwise, staves will dry above the soil line, leaving gaps that will let water escape.

Double-pot for insulation. Nest a small pot inside a larger one; then fill the space between pots with potting soil. The extra inches of soil around the inner pot keep roots cool and retard moisture loss. Plants will grow better and need watering less often than if the small pot were exposed directly to sun and wind. Keep the insulating soil moist, as well.

Use soil polymers. For maximum moisture retention, mix your potting soil with superabsorbent soil polymers. These gel-like particles act much like tiny sponges, absorbing hundreds of times their weight in water and dissolved nutrients. Plants can draw moisture directly from the polymers. Because polymers retain water that usually drains from the container, they furnish water to plant roots even when the soil itself is dry.

Conserving Water with Drip Irrigation

The advantages of using drip irrigation in the garden—the saving of both water and labor—can apply to container gardening, as well. Using one or more emitters to supply each container, you can water all of them at the same time just by turning on the water. And if your container-watering system is connected to a controller, or timer, the watering can be completed automatically, according to a programmed schedule.

Materials. Hardware stores and irrigation supply retailers offer a wide choice of emitters, tubing, and fittings. You can buy drip-irrigation components separately or purchase a packaged kit.

A drip-irrigation system for container plants resembles a garden system: you use a ½-inch tube for the main supply line and extend ¼ inch tubing from it to each pot, where you place one or more emitters.

Medium-size and larger pots will need more than one emitter to moisten all soil well. If a container needs two emitters, you can use a ¼-inch tee fitting to make a two-armed, T-shaped service line, putting an emitter at the end of each arm.

If you need more than two emitters in a large container, it's easiest to install in-line emitters, spaced where you want them in a ring of microtubing within each pot. You form a ring of tubing from a tee connection, splicing in the emitters at equal intervals around the circle.

Raising humidity. Some plants perform better in humid air. For example, bonsai plants may need to be sprinkled frequently during warm weather.

To raise humidity and mist plants easily, install a drip line set with mist emitters that disperse a fine spray of water into the air. You can purchase these emitters in a variety of outputs, from less than one gallon per hour (gph) to several gph. If the mist system is attached to a controller, it can mist your plants several times a day without any attention from you.

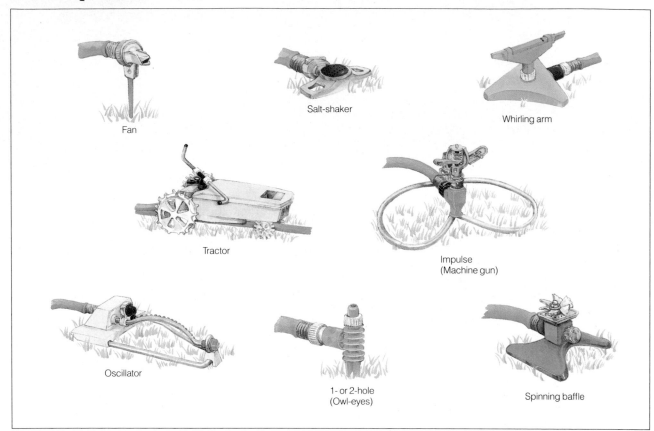

Fan

Salt-shaker

Whirling arm

Tractor

Impulse
(Machine gun)

Oscillator

1- or 2-hole
(Owl-eyes)

Spinning baffle

SPRINKLER TYPE	COVERAGE (MAX.)	PATTERN	RATE*	DISTRIBUTION
Fan	200–300 sq. ft.	Broad crescent; low arc	Fast	Light distribution from sprinkler to pattern's center, heavy from there to edge. Use this to water garden beds from the outside.
Salt-shaker	450–900 sq. ft.	Rectangle, circle; medium arc	Fast	Erratic distribution; varies from manufacturer to manufacturer, but none we tested had even distribution across whole pattern.
1- or 2-hole (Owl-eyes)	700–900 sq. ft.	Square, circle; low arc	Fast	Most are erratic, with heaviest distribution near pattern's center. Use only when impure water would clog salt-shaker sprinkler.
Spinning baffle	800–1,300 sq. ft.	Rectangle, circle, square; medium arc	Fast	Most have rapid fall-off from sprinkler to pattern edge. One, powered by a spinning plastic head, drops off only slightly from center to edge, but at high pressure the base vibrates wildly.
Whirling arm	1,000–2,000 sq. ft.	Square, circle; medium-high arc	Medium	Generally even, with a little fall-off from pattern center to edge. This is a good medium-coverage sprinkler.
Oscillator	2,000–3,000 sq. ft.	Rectangle; high arc	Medium	Conventional ones make unacceptable puddles at ends of pattern. Improved kinds shown above are very even on full pattern. Most kinds uneven on partial patterns.
Impulse (Machine gun)	5,000–6,500 sq. ft.	All or part of circle; low arc	Slow	Distributes water very evenly and is adjustable. Low arc is an advantage on windy days or for large lawns planted with trees.
Tractor	Path 50 feet wide, any length	Variable; low arc	Medium	Distributes water more heavily toward center than edge; adjustable arc. This moving sprinkler follows hose over any path you choose.

*Rate column reflects how quickly each sprinkler puts down water on an average square foot of its pattern.

charges water slowly. For lighter, sandier soils, you can use sprinklers that apply a greater volume. The chart on the facing page shows specifications for the most widely sold types.

To save water, try to match the sprinkler's spray pattern with the area you'll be watering. Choose a round pattern for spot applications—such as new plantings or dry patches in a lawn—and for areas that can be covered adequately in overlapping circles. For a rectangular area, look for a spray pattern that will match your rectangle; some models make short, squat rectangles, while others make long, narrow ones.

Remember that the different sprinkler models will deliver spray at varying heights. You'll want to choose a model that avoids interference by foliage.

Distribution patterns. Each type of sprinkler has a general pattern of water distribution, as shown on the chart on the facing page. Your goal is to achieve an even distribution of water over the entire pattern.

However, evenness of water distribution varies among the types and from one manufacturer to another. To ensure even coverage, test the water distribution of your sprinklers, then overlap their coverages to compensate for irregularities.

Testing your sprinklers. To test circular-pattern sprinklers with moving parts, set out glasses of similar size along one radius of the circle. Place the closest glass a foot from the sprinkler; space the rest at 30-inch intervals out to the edge of the pattern. To test other sprinklers, space a dozen glasses evenly over half the sprinkler's watering pattern.

Turn on the sprinklers for 30 minutes (15 minutes for high-volume ones), measure the water from each glass in a rain gauge or measuring cup, and chart the results. The glass nearest the edge of the spray pattern usually has much less water than the others, but most glasses should contain quantities within 40 percent of each other.

Fan sprinklers are an exception. Designed to water garden beds from the outside, they put most of their water well away from the sprinkler head.

Selecting a Hose

When you buy a hose, you should consider both its material and its size (inside diameter and length).

Materials. Hoses are made from rubber, unreinforced vinyl, vinyl reinforced with fiber-cord netting, and reinforced rubber-vinyl.

■ ***Rubber hoses,*** which have a dull surface, are the heaviest and toughest hoses. Although flexible, they can kink, especially when left in hot sun. They work well in cold temperatures and resist fire better than vinyl hoses.

■ ***Unreinforced vinyl hoses*** are smooth, shiny, lightweight, and inexpensive, but they are the least durable type. They kink easily, especially during extremes of cold and hot weather, and can burst if the nozzle is shut off. In freezing weather, an all-vinyl hose may become so brittle that it can break.

■ ***Reinforced vinyl hoses*** have a textured, shiny exterior. Tough and kink resistant, these hoses also are lightweight—a good choice if you need to move your hose frequently.

■ ***Reinforced rubber-vinyl hoses*** have a textured, somewhat shiny appearance. They're flexible, kink resistant, moderately heavy, and durable.

Sizes. Garden hoses are sold in varying lengths and by inside diameter; the three common hose sizes are ½ inch, ⅝ inch, and ¾ inch. (The outside diameter varies according to the hose material.) All hose ends have the same size threads.

Though the difference in hose diameters may seem slight, the water volume each can carry varies greatly. A ¾-inch-diameter hose can deliver more than twice as much water as a ½-inch hose. But when you attach a sprinkler, the difference diminishes, so that a ½-inch hose may deliver 75 or 80 percent as much water as a ¾-inch model.

If you have low water pressure (less than 30 psi) or if you must run your hose uphill (you lose 4.3 psi for every 10 feet of elevation gain), you need all the pressure and flow you can get. Buy the largest diameter, shortest hose that's practical for your situation.

Rigid-pipe Sprinkler Systems

Traditionally used for watering lawns, these underground pipe systems with risers for sprinkler heads remain the best method for watering medium-size to large lawns and low-growing ground covers. Low- and matched-precipitation-rate sprinkler heads (see page 40) make these systems more water thrifty than they once were.

However, for the greatest water economy, limit the use of rigid-pipe sprinkler head installations to lawns and some ground covers; set up the rest of your garden watering—trees, shrubs, perennials, annuals, and vegetables—with drip irrigation.

Basic Components

Regardless of the size of your underground system, you'll need to assemble standard components as discussed below. Optional additions that can improve water economy are described on page 41.

Control valves equipped with antisiphon devices, either integral or separate, operate circuits, each designed to serve plants with similar water needs. The control valves regulate the water flow from your water source to the sprinkler heads; the antisiphon valves prevent the backflow of water from sprinkler system lines into the main water line.

Residential water lines seldom possess enough water pressure to service the house as well as water an entire garden at one time. Unless you have only a small area to water, you'll need to separate your sprinkler system into several circuits, each serving only part of the lawn or garden and operated by its own control/antisiphon valve. You then operate one circuit at a time to avoid exceeding the maximum flow rate of your water supply. For circuit setup information, see pages 41–43.

Rigid polyvinyl chloride (PVC) pipe, much easier to install and longer lasting

Components of an Automatic Sprinkler System

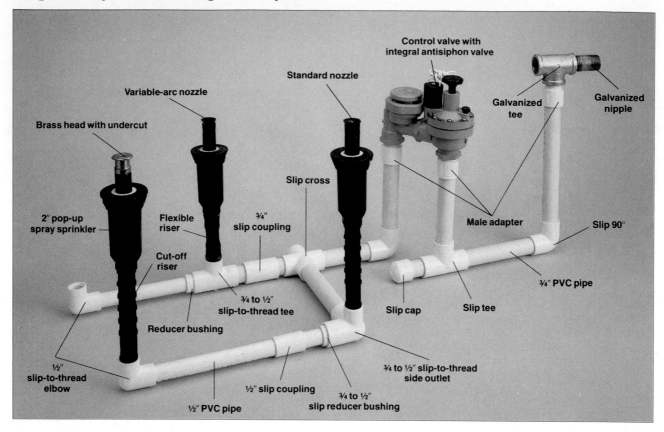

Control valve with integral antisiphon valve

Standard nozzle

Variable-arc nozzle

Brass head with undercut

Galvanized tee

Galvanized nipple

Slip cross

2" pop-up spray sprinkler

Flexible riser

¾" slip coupling

Male adapter

Slip 90°

Cut-off riser

¾" PVC pipe

¾ to ½" slip-to-thread tee

Reducer bushing

Slip cap

Slip tee

½" slip-to-thread elbow

¾ to ½" slip-to-thread side outlet

½" slip coupling

¾ to ½" slip reducer bushing

½" PVC pipe

than traditional galvanized pipe, is now the material of choice for underground watering systems. Pipes, which come in 10- or 20-foot lengths, are cut to length using pipe cutters or a hacksaw. Connections (except those to the main water line) are made using special PVC connectors and solvent cement.

PVC pipe comes with flared and standard ends. The standard end of one pipe fits into the flared end of the next, or into a fitting; solvent cement bonds the joints. The pipe comes in several strength designations. Use heavy-duty pipe where pressure is highest, and thinner, less expensive pipe for lines that are under no pressure.

For best results, choose pipe with the same diameter (or a bit larger) as the house service line, usually ¾ inch or 1 inch diameter. Manufacturers recommend a maximum of 13 gallons per minute (gpm) for ¾-inch pipe and 22 gpm for 1-inch pipe. To determine the gpm of your lines, see page 41.

PVC pipe fittings are available in an assortment of shapes that let you connect two pipes at almost any angle. You'll also find special fittings for connecting PVC pipe to galvanized pipe and to connect pipes of different sizes. Many fittings are joined to pipe with PVC solvent cement. However, some fittings— such as risers and the tees to which they join—are designed to screw together. With these fittings, always use pipe tape when making the connection.

Risers are the vertical pipe sections that connect underground pipes to sprinkler heads. The length of each riser depends on the depth of the underground pipes and the height of the sprinkler heads above the soil surface. You can buy risers in specific lengths or in continuous, threaded pieces that you cut to length. Rigid risers are most common, though you can also purchase flexible risers that will bend rather than break when hit.

Sprinkler heads are manufactured in many different spray patterns; these include full, half, and quarter circles (the traditional lawn-sprinkler heads) and rectangular spray shapes. You also can find a number of specialty heads, as described below.

The familiar sprinkler heads that produce a fountain (or partial fountain) of spray may apply water faster than the soil can absorb it. To avoid or minimize runoff, you can water in a series of short periods with a brief interval after each period. A better solution is to install low-precipitation-rate heads that deliver significantly less water per hour.

If you plan to combine full- and partial-circle heads, look for matched-precipitation-rate heads as mentioned on page 36.

Impulse (impact or machine gun) sprinklers and the multistream rotor types are useful for watering lawns and low ground covers. These sprinklers throw water 40 or more feet (depending on the model) in a moving stream; you adjust the sprinkler for coverage—from a fraction of a circle to a full 360°. You'll need fewer sprinklers to water a given area because of the distance each covers. Most apply water at a slow rate, allowing the soil to absorb moisture with little or no runoff.

If you plan to water your lawn using a system of heads laid out in a grid pattern, look for sprinklers with pop-up heads. When not in use, the head sinks below the turf surface; during sprinkling, the central core of the head thrusts above the lawn to distribute the water.

Bubbler heads are useful for watering trees and shrubs with watering basins. Bubblers produce a reduced flow of water that gurgles onto the soil.

Automated Options

The addition of electronic controls to your watering system offers two significant advantages. Watering will be done whether you are at home or not—and with no risk that you might forget. Automation also can conserve water by turning off the flow at a specific time, and by leaving the system off when the soil is moist enough.

Controllers. Hardware stores and suppliers of irrigation equipment offer a variety of electronic controllers (often called timers) that can handle gardens with diverse water needs. They range from single-program, multiple station types to complex and versatile multi-program, multistation systems.

The heart of an automatic system, the controller directs the watering cycle by automatically activating the control valves for the different circuits so they turn on for a selected (programmed) period of time, at the hour and day you choose.

Multiprogram controllers let you set up different watering frequencies and durations on different lines, so that plants with different needs receive the right amounts of water. One circuit and program might handle lawn watering, another perennials and ground covers, while a third might serve established shrubs or trees.

The most flexible (but often costlier) controller clocks are those that can be scheduled in hours, rather than just minutes, since they'll run long enough for deep watering of trees and shrubs. Less expensive is a clock that can repeat its cycle several times a day, accomplishing deep watering by using several separate waterings.

The number of control valves in your watering system determines the size controller you'll need. If you might want to add circuits later, it's a good idea to buy a controller with more station terminals than you currently need.

Most new controllers are solid state with electronic components, operating on low, 24-volt current. You also can buy battery-operated controllers to use in situations where electrical hookups are difficult or impossible.

Sensors and shutoffs. The disadvantage to automatic controllers is that they operate on preset schedules that fail to take weather into account. For example, a program set to activate a circuit every Thursday for one hour will do so even if it rains that day or the day before.

To circumvent the controller's inflexible scheduling, consider these electronic attachments:

■ **A soil moisture sensor** (also called a tensiometer, if it operates by measuring soil moisture tension) cues the controller to operate only when soil moisture is sufficiently low to warrant watering. This ensures that watering will be less frequent in cool or cloudy weather, more frequent during hot or windy spells. When a moisture sensor is linked to the system, the controller must be set to water every day; the sensor then will trigger it only when water is needed.

■ **A rain shutoff** also prevents needless watering that could occur during or soon after rainfall. You connect it to the controller, mounting a rainwater collecting pan where it will be exposed to open sky but won't accumulate leaves or other debris. When rainwater fills the collecting pan to a prescribed depth, an electric impulse shuts off the system. Once the water has evaporated from the pan, the controller is reactivated to water according to the preset schedule.

Designing Your System

Before you can plan your system, you'll need to map your property, measure your water pressure, and determine the water volume your service line can handle.

Mapping your property. Using graph paper (so you can sketch to scale), plot the location of all structures, walkways and driveways, fences, trees, and all lawn and planting areas. Be sure to indicate the spot where you intend to tap into the main water supply.

Check with your utility company if you think there may be underground utility lines on your property. If so, note them on your drawing. You also should check with the local building department to learn if a permit will be needed for the installation you plan.

Measuring water pressure. Most sprinklers won't operate efficiently when the water pressure of the water meter and service line is too low. A minimum pressure of 20 pounds per square inch (psi) usually is needed.

To measure water pressure, you'll need a pressure gauge, which you can obtain from an irrigation equipment retailer or hardware store. Measure the pressure at an outside faucet when no water is running indoors or outside. Turn the faucet completely open; then record the pressure. Repeat this at each faucet location, taking several readings at each throughout the day. In your system calculations, use the lowest pressure reading you obtain.

If you are unable to locate a pressure gauge, ask your local water company for the psi average in your neighborhood.

Determining delivery volume. To be sure your main water line can handle your proposed sprinkler system, you'll need to know the rate at which water travels through your pipes. This rate is measured in gallons per minute (gpm).

If your outdoor faucet has the same diameter as your main service line, here's the simplest way to determine the gpm rate: place a 1-gallon container under the faucet and count the number of seconds needed to fill the bucket; then divide the number of seconds into 60 to determine your line's gpm.

If your main service line has a larger diameter than the faucet, check with an irrigation equipment retailer for help in measuring your main line's gpm.

Plotting a sprinkler system. The map of your property, with structures and plantings indicated, is essential in planning the layout of your sprinkler system. From it you'll know what areas need to be watered, and you can begin to design the various circuits that will serve your landscape.

Each of the circuits will have its own control valve, allowing you to water the various garden areas—lawns, ground covers, shrubs, annual and perennial plantings—at different rates, durations, and times. Thus, each area will get no more (but no less) than the water it needs.

In designing each circuit, remember that the total gpm output of its combined sprinkler heads cannot exceed the gpm from your main water line. (If it does, your coverage will be inadequate.)

To determine a circuit's total gpm output, you must know the gpm of each sprinkler head in your proposed circuit. You can attach as many *similar* sprinklers as you want on a circuit as long as the total gpm remains less than that of the main water line.

Don't place different types of sprinkler heads on the same circuit. If you plan to use different sprinkler head types for different plantings, put the different types on separate circuits.

An individual sprinkler won't deliver an even amount of water over the area it covers, so you must overlap sprinkler spray patterns for even coverage. As a guide, separate the heads by half the diameter of their coverage. Manufacturer specifications for your sprinkler heads may give more precise spacing instructions.

If your sprinkler system contains more than one circuit, you should group all control valves into a manifold. (If you have one circuit for the front yard, and another for the backyard, this may not be practical.) With all control valves in one place, it is easy to turn on water anywhere on your property. If you plan to automate watering with a controller, the manifold makes attachment simple.

Installing a System

Laying the pipe and building the manifold are separate procedures. Once these jobs are complete, you connect the manifold to the pipe and install the risers and sprinkler heads. It's best to install a system working from the farthest pipe toward the manifold, or vice versa. But it is important to determine the location of your manifold and the tie-in to the main water line before you begin digging trenches for the lines.

Digging trenches. Lay out each trench with string and stakes. Dig it at least 8 inches deep; to avoid hand labor, you can rent a trenching machine.

Cutting and laying pipe. Assembling a system always entails some pipe cutting and fitting. First, carefully measure your pipe runs and cut the pipes with a PVC pipe cutter or hacksaw, scraping off any burrs from the cut ends with a utility knife. (To prevent dirt from getting into pipes, prop the pipe ends out of the trench when you work on them.)

You join the PVC pipes and fittings using solvent cement. Work quickly with the cement—it adheres rapidly, and cemented joints cannot be broken apart.

To make the unions, first clean the areas to be cemented with a cloth and apply primer to the surfaces that will be joined (the outside of the standard pipe end and the inside of the flared end or fitting). Then brush solvent cement evenly over the primer. Lower the pipes back into the trench, push the standard pipe end into the fitting or flared end, and rotate it about a quarter turn. Hold the pieces together for about 20 seconds until set.

When you lay the assembled pipes in the trenches, keep them as level as possible (minor variations won't cause problems) and connect pipes to the service line as described below.

Wait at least an hour (longer in cold weather) before running water through the pipes.

Connecting to the service line. Regardless of where you're tapping into the water line, be sure to turn off the main water supply to the house before you start work. In regions where soil freezes in winter, install an automatic drain valve at the low point of each circuit.

■ ***To tap in at an outside faucet,*** remove the faucet and install a 1-inch galvanized or copper tee; then reattach the faucet. Attach a male adapter to the tee, install a shutoff valve, and run pipe from the valve to the manifold.

■ ***To tap directly into the main line,*** cut out a small piece of the line and replace it with a compression tee. Then install a shutoff valve so you can turn off the water to the irrigation system and still have water to the house. (Some local codes also may require you to install an antisiphon valve.)

■ ***To tap in at a basement meter,*** cut into the service line just past the water meter. Install a compression tee and shutoff valve; then drill a hole through the basement wall above the foundation for the outgoing pipe.

Assembling and attaching the manifold. You can assemble the manifold (the grouping of control valves) on a workbench or other convenient place. On the back of each control valve, screw in a tee fitting and attach a length of PVC pipe. This pipe will connect all your control valves (space the valves at least 3 inches apart for easy access).

Then attach separate fittings to the threaded outlet in the front of each control valve. Later, you'll connect the pipes leading directly to the sprinklers to these fittings. Be sure to use fittings and pipe the same size as the control valves. If you bury the manifold to keep it out of sight, be sure to place a box around it for protection.

Finally, connect the pipes to the manifold. Use pipe tape and twist the screw fitting hand-tight only. If you use a wrench, you risk stripping the threads inside the control valve.

Test the manifold for leaks; if you find any, unscrew the fitting, dry it off, and apply new pipe tape before handscrewing it back into the control valve.

Installing risers. With a tape measure, determine the desired height of each sprinkler head. (The top of the pop-up sprinklers should be level with the finished soil.) Cut a flexible riser to that length, or use a precut riser. Then cut the pipe in the trench at each sprinkler location; install a tee fitting and attach the riser, making sure it is perpendicular to the surrounding terrain.

Flushing the system. Turn on the water, one circuit at a time. (Make sure the pipe solvent cement has had at least an hour to dry.) Check the water as it gushes out of the risers, waiting until it runs clear before you shut it off and attach sprinkler heads.

Attaching the sprinkler heads. Screw the sprinkler heads to the risers, taking care to align them properly. After you turn on the system, adjust the spray direction as needed.

Backfilling trenches. Replace the soil to a depth slightly lower than the surrounding soil. Flood the trenches with water to settle the soil; then add more soil, mounding it slightly. Sprinkle the mound for further settling.

Drip-irrigation Systems

Unlike rigid-pipe, underground sprinkler systems, which use high water pressure and volume to dispense water over a large area, drip irrigation delivers water at low pressure and volume to specific areas—often to individual plants. Penetration of water is slow, its depth regulated by the length of time the system is on.

The result is well-watered plants with less use of water than with sprinklers. Drip emitters, which release water directly to the soil, waste virtually no water; even mini-sprayers and mini-sprinklers, which spray water into the air, conserve much more water than ordinary sprinklers.

A drip-irrigation system can be connected to your main water line or operated from a hose bibb or the end of a hose. It's easy to convert an existing rigid-pipe system to a drip system, as explained on page 46.

Basic Components

A drip-irrigation system is easy to assemble and simple to modify. Most systems are made from polyethylene tubing fitted with emitters or sprays. You'll find materials at irrigation supply retailers and at many hardware stores.

Tubing. The standard way to distribute water is through ½- or ⅜-inch flexible black polyethylene tubing attached with plastic fittings and laid on the surface of the soil (where it can be obscured by a mulch) or concealed just slightly beneath the surface. For a sturdy but less flexible system, you can use buried PVC pipe for main lines and polyethylene tubing for lateral lines. For more information, see page 46.

Emitters, sprayers, and soakers. You can choose from a variety of emitters, all of which deliver water slowly, through small openings at prescribed low rates.

In addition to the various emitters, you have a choice of mini-sprayers, mini-sprinklers, and soaker tubing, allowing you great latitude in design.

Emitters can be set directly into the main line. More often, however, you run thin, ¼-inch microtubing—often referred to as spaghetti tubing—from the main line to individual plants and then attach emitters to the microtubing.

If your system includes underground PVC pipe (see page 39), you can incorporate multioutlet emitters with up to six outlets per head. You screw an emitter onto a PVC riser, then attach microtubing to extend to individual plants.

Most emitters and sprayers have barbed ends that snap into ½- and ⅜-inch poly tubing or push into microtubing. Some are barbed on both ends so that you can create a chain or circle of in-line emitters on microtubing.

Pressure-compensating emitters provide a steady flow rate despite low or high pressure from the tap. Use these emitters if your setup spans an elevation

Components of a Drip-irrigation System

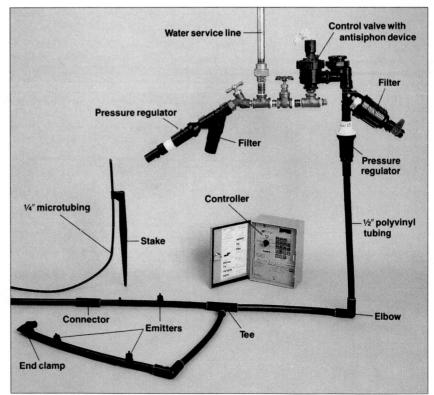

For these plants...	In this soil...	Use this many emitters
LOW SHRUBS	Sandy soil	One 2-gph emitter next to plant
	Loam soil	One 1-gph emitter next to plant
	Clay soil	One ½-gph emitter next to plant
MEDIUM TO LARGE SHRUBS	Sandy soil	Two or three 2-gph emitters placed evenly around plant
	Loam soil	Two or three 1-gph emitters placed evenly around plant
	Clay soil	Two or three ½-gph emitters placed evenly around plant
SMALL TREES (6- TO 8-FOOT-WIDE CANOPY)	Sandy soil	Three to six 1-gph emitters or two or three 2-gph emitters, installed on a J-loop or on two lines set on opposite sides of the trunk
	Loam soil	Two or three 1-gph emitters, installed as above
	Clay soil	Two or three ½-gph emitters, installed as above
LARGER TREES (10- TO 15-FOOT DIAMETER)	Sandy soil	Four to ten 2-gph emitters, installed on a J-loop or on two lines on opposite sides of the trunk
	Loam soil	Four to ten 1-gph emitters (or three to six 2-gph), installed as above
	Clay soil	Four to ten ½-gph or three to six 1-gph emitters, installed as above
GROUND COVERS SPACED AT LEAST 2 FEET APART	Sandy or loam soil	One 1-gph emitter at rootball
	Clay soil	One ½-gph emitter at rootball
CLOSER GROUND COVERS WITH LESS DISTINCT ROOT ZONES	Any soil	Overlapping mini-sprays or sprinklers (or see below)
BEDS OF FLOWERS, GROUND COVERS, OR VEGETABLES	Sandy soil	Several 2-gph emitters spaced about a foot apart in a row
	Loam soil	Several 1-gph emitters spaced about 1½ feet apart in a row
	Clay soil	Several ½-gph emitters spaced about 1½ feet apart in a row
CONTAINER PLANTS	Potting soil	One or more ½- or 1-gph emitters, depending on pot size

change greater than 10 feet, if lateral lines exceed 200 feet, or if emitters on a line add up to more than 100 gallons per hour (gph).

■ **Drip emitters** are best for watering individual plants, such as trees, shrubs, some vines, and perennials. Water placement is more precise than with mini-sprayers or mini-sprinklers, and the emitters can be hidden from view.

■ **Diaphragm-type emitters** have an interior diaphragm that opens or closes to control flow as pressure changes. These emitters are usually pressure compensating and self-flushing (the diaphragm opens at the start and end of a cycle to flush out particles). Diaphragm-type emitters are best for hilly and sloping land, and for systems that use long lines of emitters.

■ **Turbulent-flow emitters** have twisting internal pathways that reduce pressure by creating turbulence, which also makes them partially pressure compensating. The wide channels can pass debris, so this type of emitter is less likely to clog, an important consideration when water quality is poor.

■ **Vortex-type emitters** spin water in interior chambers to lower pressure where the water exits. If water passing through them is high in calcium, these emitters tend to clog.

Mini-sprayers, mini-sprinklers, and misters spread water over a wider area than emitters, but they still operate at low flow rates and low pressure. Use them where soil is heavily infiltrated by roots—such as ground covers that root along stems as they spread, and mixed annual and perennial plantings.

■ **Mini-sprayers** are available in various spray patterns—from full circle to a fraction of a circle—so you can use them in tight or irregularly shaped spaces. The radius of coverage ranges from 4 to 10 feet; water output varies from 3 to 30 gallons per hour (gph).

■ **Mini-sprinklers** emit larger droplets than mini-sprayers, so they're less affected by wind. All give full-circle coverage (with a radius from 10 to 30 feet) at outputs from 3 to 30 gph.

■ **Misters** deliver a very fine spray at a low output (2 to 5 gph). Use them with ferns, bonsai, and other plants that require high humidity and/or frequent light waterings. Because the fine water droplets are easily dispersed by wind, use misters in protected areas or early in the morning when the air is still.

Perforated and porous pipes act as linear drip emitters, oozing water along their entire lengths.

■ **Perforated pipe** (sometimes called soaker hose) emits water through tiny holes spaced at precise intervals; often the holes are laser-drilled (hence another name, laser tubing). You'll find it useful for vegetable and flower plantings (particularly for row crops) that are replaced annually or every few years.

It's best not to rely on the pipe for watering permanent shrubs and trees, though; eventually, the holes tend to clog, and they can't be reopened as most clogged emitters can. A good filter is essential.

■ **Porous pipe,** from which water oozes through pores along its length, is best used in underground installations where the tubing will stay constantly moist. If the pipe dries out between watering cycles, calcium may build up inside and clog the pores. It works best at very low pressure: 5 to 10 psi.

Valves. You'll need a valve to turn water on and off. If you design a hose-end or hose-bibb system, you'll use the hose bibb. But if you connect directly to your water line, you'll need a control/anti-siphon valve as described on page 39.

Filter. Particulate impurities in water are the main enemy of drip systems. A good filter, installed just below the control/antisiphon valve, will save you the time and frustration of cleaning clogged emitters.

A Y-filter with 150- to 200-mesh fiberglass or stainless steel screen is best for systems connected directly to a water source. For hose-bibb or hose-end systems, connect an in-line filter directly to the hose bibb; then add a pressure regulator (see below) and attach the system's main feeder line to it or to the end of a hose that connects between the pressure regulator and the drip system.

Pressure regulator. Low-volume systems are designed to operate best at water pressures between 20 and 30 pounds per square inch (psi). However, many household water lines operate at higher pressures. To learn the pressure in your household water lines, refer to page 41.

For best performance, most drip-irrigation systems need a pressure reg-ulator, installed between the filter and the main drip line. Preset to 20 or 30 psi, the regulator reduces pressure to a rate that the system can accept.

Optional Equipment

Several other devices can be incorporated into a drip system. Controllers, sensors, and shutoff valves are described on page 41.

Fertilizer injectors are particularly useful with drip-irrigation systems, where water is applied directly to the soil. A fertilizer injector will add liquid fertilizer to your watering system. You have a choice of two types.

For hose end drip systems, you can use either a cartridge attachment that holds special dry but soluble fertilizers or a siphon-attachment injector that sucks liquid fertilizer concentrate from a bucket and puts it into the system. Both devices attach between the hose bibb and the filter.

For drip systems connected directly to your household water line, you can install a fertilizer-injector canister in each system between the control/antisiphon valve and the filter. The canister accommodates either dissolved dry fertilizer or liquid fertilizer (but not fish emulsion, which can clog emitters).

Design & Assembly

Advance planning is crucial to the success of a drip-irrigation system. Begin with an overall concept, then progress to layout of lines, choice of emitters, and determination of the number of emitters to be installed on each line or system. Be sure you know your garden's soil type (see pages 29–30), since water will move differently through different kinds of soils.

Planning your system. Sketch on paper the area or areas you want served (as described on page 41), pencil in any obstacles between the water source and the area, such as patios and walkways. Also mark any slopes or elevation changes, as these can affect water dis-

Measuring Soil Moisture

You've watered your garden, but how wet is it? A moisture sensor or soil probe will show you just how deeply water is penetrating the earth.

Moisture sensors. These instruments gauge the soil's moisture content in several ways. Some sensors are portable; you insert the instrument anywhere in the garden you want to test for soil moisture. Others are intended for permanent installation, giving you a reading in prescribed, fixed locations.

The device that measures moisture tension is called a tensiometer; it's a sealed, water-filled metal tube with a porous ceramic tip at one end and a pressure gauge at the opposite end. Other sensors measure temperature or the electrical conductivity of the soil.

Be sure to place a sensor in a spot representative of the area you're watering. You may want to take readings from locations that appear to dry out first.

Soil probes. Although less sophisticated than moisture sensors, soil probes can tell you when to water—some by letting you see what is happening underground.

Soil-sampling tubes pull out a plug of soil so you can see moisture content in a cross section. To help determine if you're watering enough, push a sampling tube into the soil about 24 hours after watering (you can't get a good core in mud or dry soil). If the core is moist only 2 inches deep and you want to wet the soil to 12 inches, you know you'll need to water about six times as long. Repeat the test in several areas of a planting.

A soil core also can indicate when it's time to water again by revealing the depth of dry soil from the surface downward.

A screwdriver, or even a stiff wire, can give you a rough reading of moisture penetration. Simply poke the screwdriver or wire into the soil in several places. It will penetrate easily throughout the depth of moist soil.

tribution and choice of certain components.

Next, determine the flow rate of water from your garden faucet (for directions, see page 41). From this figure, you can calculate the number of emitters you can place on one line, remembering that the emitters' total output (in gph) should not exceed 75 percent of available water flow at the faucet.

Laying out lines. Group plants with differing water needs on separate systems; if your systems are connected directly to the household water lines, use separate control valves. Be careful not to run lines too long or to put too many emitters on one line: the tubing has limits on how much water it can efficiently handle. Remember that running a line uphill shortens the possible run, downhill increases it. (For more information about running lines on slopes, see at right.)

You can either bury the lines 2 to 3 inches in the soil or leave them on the surface. Buried lines last longer, are less prone to disturbance, and don't affect the appearance of your garden. But lines left on the surface are easier to install, repair, and maintain. If you add a 2-inch layer of mulch over surface lines, you create many of the same benefits that you have with buried lines.

Choosing and spacing emitters. The number and gallonage of emitters you use for each plant will depend on your soil and the plants you're watering.

As a rule of thumb, use higher-gpm emitters for plants in sandy soil and lower-gpm emitters for plants in clay soil. For shallow-rooted plants, space emitters closer together. Refer to the chart on page 44 for guidelines.

Spacing of emitters is greatly affected by the layout of plants. If perennials or woody plants are placed less than about 2 feet apart in a confined bed, there's no need to design a system to suit each plant: the bed will eventually fill up with roots. Simply space emitters 1½ to 2 feet apart to moisten the entire planting.

For established trees and shrubs, place the emitters about one-third to one-half the distance between the trunk and the drip line. You may have to adjust placement of emitters or sprays for maximum efficiency. (For example, a shrub might need only one emitter instead of two because an emitter on a neighboring tree is wetting part of its roots.)

Systematizing a slope. Gravity slows the flow of water uphill and speeds it downhill. Therefore, if your lines will run on a hillside or bank, set the control/antisiphon valves at the top of the slope. Run main lines perpendicular to the slope and lateral lines parallel to it.

If you will be installing drip emitters, be sure to use the pressure-compensating kind. When you plan to use mini-sprayers, choose half-circle sprays and position them so they spray downhill.

Installing a drip system. To assemble a drip-irrigation system, you'll need some simple tools: pruning shears to cut tubing, a special hole-punching device to install emitters, and a number of hairpin anchor stakes to secure the tubing to the ground.

Following the order of components as illustrated on page 43, assemble the valve(s), filter, and pressure regulator. If you're connecting the system directly to a water line, install a shutoff valve between the water line and your system; this will allow you to shut off the irrigation system but still use any other outlet from the main line.

Wrap threaded connections with pipe tape before attaching them. Hand-tighten plastic fittings. Make sure the arrows on valves and pressure regulators point in the direction of water flow.

Connect the tubing to the valve assembly and lay out the main distribution lines; whenever possible, place them next to walls and edges of paths where they'll be easy to find and more protected from disturbance. Then attach lateral lines with tee and elbow fittings. Use hairpin stakes to secure all tubing in place. Run water through the lines to flush out dirt.

To punch holes in the tubing for emitters or microtubing, hold the hole punch perpendicular to the tubing, squeeze the tube on each side with your fingers to keep it from flattening, and then push and twist straight down.

Once the system is assembled, flush the lines again, close off the ends, and then turn it on. To confirm that you have enough emitters in the right places, let the system run for its normal cycle, wait several hours, then dig into the soil in several places to check the spread of moisture. If necessary, add or reposition some of the emitters.

Converting a rigid-pipe system. It is simple to convert a rigid-pipe sprinkler system to drip irrigation. First, you position a filter and pressure regulator, then retrofit one riser and cap the rest. Finally, you set up a drip-irrigation system from the one retrofitted riser. (NOTE: You must convert the system totally; drip emitters and regular sprinklers won't operate properly on one line.)

You can install the filter and pressure regulator at any riser or at the valve. In either case, you must have an antisiphon device at the valve (see page 39).

Placing the filter and pressure regulator at a riser is the easier method. Just remove all sprinkler heads, install an in-line filter and pressure regulator at one riser, then cap the other risers.

But sometimes you'll need a valve installation—if, for example, your sprinkler system waters plantings on both sides of a pavement barrier. In such cases, convert two risers—one on either side of the barrier. The filter and pressure regulator installed at the valve then function for both of the converted risers.

Anticipate the Future

As permanent, woody plants grow, you may need to add emitters to accommodate their larger root systems. To encourage deep rooting, you can change emitters to a higher output (as from 1 gph to 2 gph for trees), or you can increase the flow time period.

To allow for root growth of trees, install emitters on J-loops of ½-inch tubing around the trunks. At planting time, place the encircling line on the rootball. As trees grow, you open up the loops and add more emitters; eventually you may need to extend the tubing.

The Water-efficient Lawn

Recent studies have shown that most home gardeners routinely overwater their lawns, providing up to twice as much water as the lawns actually need. Not only is overwatering wasteful, but it also leaches fertilizers out of the root zone quickly, causing grass to grow more rapidly (which means more frequent cutting). Overwatering can also encourage diseases.

However, an underwatered lawn is both unhealthy and unattractive.

To achieve a happy medium, follow the guidelines below and heed the suggestions under "Reconsider the lawn" on page 36.

Watering Practices

Deep watering is the most effective way to water your lawn. Soak the soil deeply, then don't water again until the top inch or two begins to dry. Deep watering encourages grass roots to grow deeper into the soil; deep roots mean the turf will be less affected by surface drying.

Use soil probes or moisture sensors (see page 45) to check water penetration. If the top inch or two of soil is dry, it's time to water.

Loss of resiliency also indicates that your lawn needs water. Walk across the lawn; if your footprints remain for more than a few seconds, you need to water. Another sign that your lawn needs water is a dull appearance; the grass blades may have folded up, exposing their bases.

Water early in the morning, when little moisture will be lost to evaporation or wind. Water pressure usually is highest at that time, too. If you water at night, it keeps evaporation loss down, but a wet lawn overnight encourages pests and disease organisms.

If water runoff occurs, the problem may be your soil or the lawn, itself. Water penetrates slowly in heavy, claylike soils (see page 30). One solution is to divide the total watering period into several shorter intervals, leaving time between them for water to soak in. Another solution is to aerate your lawn; by removing plugs of soil, you provide easier entry for water.

Some lawns actually repel water because of a buildup of thatch (dead stems and blades) beneath their green surface. Dethatching such a lawn lets water reach the soil more easily.

Amount & Timing

How much water does your lawn use? The surest answer comes from learning its evapotranspiration (ET) rate. Calculated either in inches or millimeters, ET is the amount of water that evaporates from the soil plus the amount that transpires through the blades of grass. It's not an easy figure to determine; but if you can figure out the amount of water that leaves your soil, you will then know how much you need to replace.

Many communities, especially in regions of low summer rainfall, offer local watering guidelines based on ET figures. To learn if there's an ET chart for your area, contact your local water utility or County Cooperative Extension Office.

ET varies not only from place to place, but also from day to day, season to season, even year to year. Your own lawn has its individual mix of grasses, soil, slope, shade, orientation, and thatch. Even so, if you know the seasonal ET averages for your area, you can water much more efficiently. Take your garden conditions into account, and adjust your watering times with the changing seasons.

Start your ET-based lawn watering by following the recommendations in your local ET chart for the appropriate time of year. Observe your lawn for a few weeks, checking for signs of drying. If the lawn does dry before the next suggested watering, either water for slightly longer periods or for shorter but more frequent periods.

Take the weather into account: clear skies and high temperatures (especially when it's windy) affect ET more than any other factor. You'll need to water more frequently. On the other hand, periods of rainfall or cool, cloudy weather may let you stretch watering intervals. Pay close attention to your lawn's diminishing needs as weather turns cool in fall.

The Lawn Audit

To use an ET chart, you'll need to learn how much water your lawn receives from your watering system.

First, place a grid of equal-size, straight-sided containers (coffee mugs will do) at random points around your lawn. Then operate your watering system for 15 minutes. Shut off the system and measure water depth in each container.

If you find more than a ¼-inch difference in depth between containers, you should consider adjusting or changing sprinkler heads, or changing the sprinkler positions if you're using hose-end sprinklers. When you achieve a more even watering pattern, rerun the audit and use the lowest depth figure in reading an ET chart.

Although ET charts often recommend watering twice a week, short sprinklings at more frequent intervals may be preferable in extremely hot, dry climates, in very sandy soil, and in shallow-rooted lawns.

Waterwise Maintenance Practices

Every garden requires periodic maintenance—mulching, weed and pest control, fertilizing, pruning—but chores and routines vary depending on the garden's size and the plants in it.

When water conservation is a primary goal, however, you should be sure to include several specific tasks in your regular schedule of maintenance.

Mulching & Mulches

The traditional mulch is simply a layer of loose-textured organic material, from 1 to 4 inches thick, spread over the soil. The mulch layer slows the rate of evaporation from the moist soil beneath, so soil remains moist for a longer period after watering. In hot weather, a mulch also helps lower soil temperature beneath its blanket.

Because mulch moderates the extremes of moisture and temperature, it improves conditions that favor good, steady root growth. Less water is lost through evaporation, and plants perform better.

In addition, a mulch minimizes erosion and gullying by intercepting and diffusing the force of rainfall or irrigation water. Instead of scouring the bare earth and running off, the water seeps through the mulch and soaks into the ground beneath—a benefit especially important on sloping sites.

A mulch also suppresses weed growth by effectively burying seeds and discouraging their germination. If any weeds do come up in the mulch, you can pull them easily due to the mulch's loose texture. As it decomposes, the mulch improves the composition of the top few inches of soil, allowing water to penetrate the soil more easily.

Attractive bark mulch retards evaporation of moisture from soil while unifying a landscape of diverse water-conservative plants. Prominent ornamental grass is fountain grass (Pennisetum setaceum).

Wood products, sold either by the bag or in bulk, are popular materials for mulching. Finest texture is aged sawdust (left). Shredded bark (center) has natural appearance, consisting of irregularly sized pieces. Coarse bark chips (right) are available in sizes ranging from ¼ inch to 2½ inches.

Organic Mulch Materials

Gardeners have a wide choice among potential mulch materials—from coarse to fine-textured products, and from long-lasting materials to those that decompose rapidly. Among the factors governing your choice are cost, appearance, longevity, and local availability.

You'll need to calculate the amount of material you require. A 2-cubic-foot bag of packaged mulch material will cover an area of 8 square feet about 3 inches deep. If you plan to use bulk materials, estimate that one cubic yard (27 cubic feet) will cover 108 square feet with a 3-inch-deep layer of mulch. Three cubic yards will cover 1,000 square feet about 1 inch deep.

The most widely available mulch materials are described below. As you shop around, you'll probably encounter additional products as well. Whatever your choice, avoid thin-textured materials (maple leaves, for example); when wet, they pack down into a sodden mass that will repel water rather than allowing it to soak into the soil.

Wood products. Available bagged or in bulk form, products such as ground bark and sawdust are widely used as mulch. Long lasting and attractive, ground bark may be from fir, pine, hemlock, or redwood trees in tones of brown aging to gray; you can purchase bark ground, shredded, or in chips to 2½ inches. Redwood bark is the most durable.

Fine-textured fresh sawdust and wood shavings need nitrogen to decompose; if sufficient nitrogen is not present in the mulch, it will be drawn from nitrogen in the soil (needed for plants' root growth). Commercially packaged sawdust usually is fortified with nitrogen; check the package label to be sure. But if you use bulk raw sawdust or shavings as a mulch, you must add a nitrogen supplement. Apply 1 pound of actual nitrogen for every 100 square feet of mulch spread 1 inch deep. Best to use is a slow-release nitrogen fertilizer, such as ureaform (38-0-0).

Straw. Although short lived and coarse textured, straw is reasonably attractive, inexpensive, and widely available in bales. It's virtually free of weed seeds—in contrast to the similar-appearing hay, which can introduce a host of weeds into your garden.

Animal manures. Also widely available, manure is sold both commercially packaged and in bulk. When used as a mulch, its effective lifetime is about a year. Apply only aged or composted manures; fresh material can burn plant roots. Many manures (and mushroom compost, mentioned below) contain a high level of salts, which can damage plants. The best time to apply manure is just before the rainy season begins, so that rainfall can help to leach out the salts.

Agricultural by-products. These vary by region, and lasting quality depends on the material. Most are sold in bulk rather than packaged. Among by-products used as mulches are ground corncobs, mushroom compost, apple or grape pomace, hulls from various nut crops, and cotton gin waste.

Pine needles. Appearance is pleasant, permeability is excellent, and the needles will last for several years. Acid reaction may be a bonus in all but acid-soil regions.

Grass clippings. If not spread carefully and allowed to dry out, grass clippings may compact into a smelly, water-repellent mat. Start by spreading a thin layer (½ to 1 inch thick) of clippings; then let this layer dry before adding another thin layer.

Tree leaves. If you want to use leaves as a mulch, choose those with thicker textures (such as the leaves of many oaks). Thin-textured leaves (notably those from maple) will mat together when spread in layers and moistened. One drawback: Most leaves can be blown around by the wind.

Inorganic Mulches

Two other materials, plastic and rock, are used as mulches in some situations. They help conserve water, as do organic mulches, but they provide no benefits to the soil.

Polypropylene plastic. Often called landscape fabric, this plastic material is laid on the bare earth. Air, water, and dissolved nutrients pass freely through the material, but the plastic suppresses weed growth. The material is particularly useful on sloping ground, where it helps to limit runoff and erosion. Available in rolls, the plastic comes in widths from 3 feet to 12 feet.

Installation is simple: you roll out the plastic on the ground, cutting it with scissors to fit around trees, shrubs, or other obstacles. For best garden appearance, cover the plastic with one of the organic mulches described above. With such a covering, the plastic will last for several years before it deteriorates.

Polyethylene plastic. Black polyethylene plastic has been used for many years as an inexpensive, easy-to-install mulch for weed suppression. Though the plastic is unattractive, its appearance can be masked by a thin layer of organic mulch material.

But unlike the polypropylene plastic fabric described above, black plastic sheeting is impermeable to water. You must deliberately punch holes in it or leave gaps between separate sheets to allow water to soak into the soil. And because the plastic tends to shed water, its use is limited to flat ground.

If you use black plastic as a weed-suppressing mulch, make sure to set plants slightly higher than the surrounding soil; otherwise, excess water will continually run off the plastic onto the plants' bases, leading to root rot from overmoist soil.

Black plastic also restricts passage of air to the soil; if plant roots are deprived of air, growth will be slowed or stopped. In addition to punching holes in the plastic, be sure to leave several inches of open soil around tree and shrub bases and to overlap seams no more than 4 inches.

Rocks. When used as an attractive element in your landscape design, rocks become a permeable and permanent "mulch" to retard loss of soil moisture and prevent the germination of weed seeds from the soil beneath. You can purchase rocks of varying sizes, shapes, and colors at landscape supply firms; among the most attractive are river rocks, with rounded contours and muted colors. Unlike organic mulches, rocks will need periodic grooming to remove accumulated litter that detracts from their appearance.

Weed Control

When you're trying to conserve water in your garden, weeds become more than an unattractive nuisance. Because they're growing, they're stealing water from any ornamental plants nearby. In a water-thrifty garden, especially, weed suppression and eradication are of major importance.

It's impossible to completely banish weeds from your garden, because the seeds are carried by wind, birds, and muddy feet. Eternal vigilance is the key to weed control. Immediately eliminate any weeds before they produce seeds that will spawn an even larger crop the next year.

You can attack weeds in several ways, depending on the extent of the problem and available time.

Hand methods. The oldest weed control method involves simply removing the offenders by hand—by hand-pulling, hoeing, or tilling.

Hand-pulling is an efficient way to eliminate a few stray weeds; hoeing or tilling can effectively clear an area prior to planting. But if you need to eliminate many weeds from a large area, it's more efficient to use an herbicide.

Herbicides. Chemical preparations that attack weeds can be a tremendous help *if* they're used with extreme caution. Be sure to choose the right herbicide for the job; you must read product labels carefully to learn which weeds the herbicide controls and on which plants the chemicals can be used without damage. *It's very important to observe all stated directions and cautions without exception.* If you use herbicides carelessly, you may seriously damage or kill ornamental plants—or fail to rid your garden of weeds.

Herbicides fall into two general categories:

Preemergence herbicides, available in granular and concentrated liquid forms, kill weed seeds just as they germinate. To be effective, these products must be applied to tilled soil that has been cleared of weeds. After applying the herbicide, you water the treated area to encourage germination and activate the herbicide. Preemergents are safe for use among many ornamental plants, but you should check each product label to confirm that it's appropriate for use among the particular plants in your garden.

Postemergence herbicides eliminate growing weeds; the specific weeds targeted by a product are noted on the product label. Many of these herbicides were developed to control weeds in grass lawns; others, especially those containing glyphosate or amino triazole, will eliminate a wide range of plant pests, including woody types such as poison oak and poison ivy.

Most postemergents are liquid concentrates that you dilute with water, then apply as a spray; some are sold prediluted in their own applicator containers—handy for spot-treatments. If you dilute the weed killer yourself, always keep a separate sprayer exclusively for it; even a small residue of herbicide can contaminate your other sprays, with potentially damaging results for ornamental plants. Always spray when the air is still, so the mist of herbicide won't be carried to nontarget plants.

Mulches. As discussed on page 49, a mulch helps control weeds by covering their seeds too deeply to allow germination. Therefore, a mulch is the logical follow-up to any weed eradication campaign, both for future weed control and for moisture conservation.

Other Garden Maintenance

Routine garden maintenance tasks also include fertilizing, pest control, pruning, and lawn mowing. Below are ways these tasks—and the way you do them—can contribute to your water-efficient garden.

Fertilizing

Applications of fertilizer—particularly nitrogen fertilizers—promote growth. Where water conservation is your goal, you may question whether fertilizing is desirable, assuming that more growth will only create a demand for more water.

Moderation is the answer. The most important role of fertilizers is in maintaining plant health—and increased growth is only one sign of health. Your goal is an attractive garden with reduced water needs, and healthy plants make an attractive garden.

Vegetable crops and some annual flowers need fertilizers for satisfying production, but don't strive for the largest tomatoes or zinnias. For your basic garden plants—trees, shrubs, vines, and perennials—fertilize as needed, when new growth is less or smaller than normal or if its color is too pale.

Pest & Disease Control

Keeping in mind that healthy plants make an attractive garden, you'll need to take timely action to control garden pests and diseases whenever a problem threatens to do significant damage. In times of severe water shortage, be especially vigilant for garden pests (such as mites, mealybugs, thrips, borers, and bark beetles); drought-stressed plants are often more vulnerable to attack.

The words "timely" and "significant damage" are important. Identify the pest or disease, and assess what harm it might do to your plants. Be willing to accept minor, casual damage; natural predators can control (but not eradicate) a number of garden pests. But if a serious problem develops, control the pest or plant disease before it spreads.

When you decide control measures are needed, try mechanical methods first. These include hand-picking, setting out various traps and barriers, and using jets of water from the hose to wash off and kill pests. If you plan to spray for pest or disease control, consider nonchemical preparations first. These include insecticidal soaps, botanical insecticides (such as pyrethrins), horticultural oils, and—for caterpillars—Bacillus thuringiensis (BT).

Should you decide stronger chemical controls are called for—often needed in disease management and spider mite control—be sure you have identified the problem correctly. Then purchase a control that is effective against the specific problem, and use it according to all cautions and directions on the product label. If you have any questions, check with a reputable local nursery or contact your County Cooperative Extension Office.

Pruning

A well-planned, healthy, water-conserving garden will need only occasional pruning to shape its plants. As the need arises, you'll prune to control wayward growth and to thin out superfluous or unproductive stems and branches. But a water-efficient garden involves no list of special pruning rules.

During a severe water shortage, don't cut back plants to reduce foliage, thinking that a smaller plant will use less water. The root system has grown to support the larger plant. Heavy pruning may stimulate vigorous new growth, which will be more vulnerable to water stress than the mature growth that was removed. Heavy pruning also may expose formerly shaded limbs to full sun, increasing the risk of damage from sunburn.

Lawn Mowing

Although lawn experts disagree on whether raising the mowing height of a lawn will reduce its water consumption, most agree that cutting a lawn at the highest allowable height for that species will result in a more extensive root system. In turn, a larger, well-developed root system is better able to withstand dry periods and to survive longer between waterings.

For bluegrass lawns, set your lawn mower to cut at 2 to 2½ inches high; for tall fescue, set it at 2½ to 3 inches. Cut warm-season grasses (such as Bermuda and zoysia) to a height of 1 inch.

Caring for Water Systems

Although you probably consider your sprinkler or drip-irrigation system as a permanent garden fixture, it nevertheless will need periodic checking and maintenance.

Rigid-pipe Sprinkler Systems

During the seasons when your system is in use, check the sprinklers monthly (or more frequently) for clogged or broken heads. Also routinely watch for any evidence of leaks and for uneven watering patterns.

Cleaning clogged sprinkler heads. When a sprinkler head is clogged, the water is forced out at an odd angle, or the amount of spray is greatly reduced.

To clean a spray-pattern sprinkler, run a knife blade through the slit in the head where water is sprayed. If it remains clogged, remove the head and clean it, being sure no dirt or debris enters the riser.

To clean an impact-type head, first run a wire down the hole where water is emitted. If further work is necessary, remove the head for a more thorough cleaning.

Replacing broken sprinklers and risers. To replace a broken sprinkler head, you'll need to remove it by hand or with a wrench and replace it with another of the same kind.

A broken riser may be difficult to extract; if so, use a stub wrench for additional leverage. If solvent cement was used to install the riser, cut the riser pipe off cleanly and attach a new riser using an adaptor fitting.

Work carefully so no soil spills into the line. If soil does enter the line, remove all sprinkler heads on the circuit. Let water gush out of the open risers until it runs clear.

Drip-irrigation Systems

Regular maintenance is the key to keeping a drip-irrigation system in good working order. The entire system should be checked at the beginning of the growing season and at least once during each season that it's used. If your water contains sediment or mineral salts, check more frequently.

Each year before use begins, open the system's end caps and flush the main and lateral lines for 2 to 5 minutes to wash accumulated sediments out of the lines. If your water is fairly clean, flush the lines every 4 to 6 months.

It's important to keep the filter clean at all times. If your water is high in sediments, check the filter frequently—as often as after each use. If you have in-line filters, remove the filter screen and wash it under running water; if the screen gets damaged or torn, replace it. The larger Y-filters, used in permanent hook-ups, can be flushed in place; if the screen becomes clogged, remove it and wash it under a faucet.

When you start up a system—whether a new one or an established setup at the start of the growing season—check the emitters after the first couple of uses. Be sure that water is flowing through them and that the wetting pattern is as expected. If no water flows through, check for one of these problems: the emitter's shutoff valve may be in the "off" position, or the emitter is plugged. You should pull out a plugged emitter and clean it; when cleaning fails to correct the problem, replace with a new emitter.

Throughout the season, you should periodically check your system for clogged or malfunctioning emitters. If you live in a region where winter temperatures normally drop below freezing, drain the system at the end of the growing season before the onset of freezing weather.

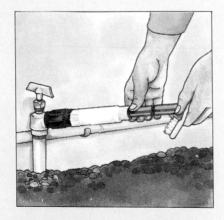

To clean an in-line filter, remove the cylindrical filter screen and wash it in running water; use a toothbrush, if needed, to remove accumulated particles.

Y-filter, commonly used in permanent drip-irrigation installations, is designed to be self-cleaning by the turn of a valve. Remove and wash filter screen only if clogging is severe.

Plants at a Glance

Creating a landscape using water-thrifty plants offers both an enjoyable gardening challenge and long-term benefits. Choosing native plants and others suited to your climate, you can develop a handsome garden filled with greenery and color. By relying heavily on these plants, you can reduce both the frequency of watering and the amount of water used. This not only conserves water but also lowers your water bill.

On the following pages, you'll find selective listings of water-conserving plants that solve common landscape needs: plants for seasonal flower color, patio and shade trees, choices suitable for shaded gardens, plants for hillsides, durable ground covers, screen and background shrubs, and climate-adapted turfgrasses. You'll also discover plants that treat specific needs, such as erosion control and wind control.

On pages 64–93, you'll find a listing of more than 350 water-thrifty trees, shrubs, vines, and perennials—plants that you can use to establish a permanently attractive and varied framework for your garden.

In this encyclopedia, plants are listed alphabetically by botanical name. Brief descriptions include each plant's common name and details of its appearance, size, water needs, and climate adaptability.

A low water budget still can buy plenty of color. Bougainvillea 'Tahitian Dawn' transforms plain garden wall into a brilliant mural; sea lavender (Limonium perezii) provides a purple accent at base of wall.

Seasonal Color

By carefully choosing the plants for your water-thrifty garden, you can enjoy lively color throughout the year. Select your plants according to their bloom season and color. Some offer flamboyant floral displays, others are more restrained.

Rudbeckia hirta

Ceanothus

NAME OF PLANT	SPRING	SUMMER	FALL	WINTER	FLOWER COLORS
Trees					
Acacia baileyana				■	Yellow
Callistemon citrinus	■	■	■	■	Red
Caragana arborescens	■				Yellow
Cercidium floridum	■				Yellow
Chilopsis linearis	■	■			White, pink
Chitalpa	■	■	■		Pink
Eucalyptus		■			Cream, pink, red
Grevillea robusta	■				Orange
Jacaranda mimosifolia	■	■			Lavender, white
Koelreuteria paniculata		■			Yellow
Lagerstroemia indica		■			White, pink, purple
Metrosideros excelsus	■	■			Red
Parkinsonia aculeata	■				Yellow
Robinia	■				White, pink
Sophora secundiflora	■			■	Violet blue
Shrubs					
Alyogyne huegelii	■	■	■		Blue
Caesalpinia	■	■			Yellow, red
Caryopteris clandonensis			■	■	Blue
Cassia artemisioides	■			■	Yellow
Ceanothus	■				Blue
Cistus	■	■			White, pink, purple
Cytisus	■				Yellow

NAME OF PLANT	SPRING	SUMMER	FALL	WINTER	FLOWER COLORS
Shrubs (cont'd)					
Escallonia	■	■	■		White, pink, red
Fremontodendron	■				Yellow
Genista	■				Yellow
Grevillea 'Noellii'	■				Pink white
Hibiscus syriacus		■			Various
Hypericum calycinum	■	■			Yellow
Lantana	■	■			Various
Lavandula	■	■	■		Lavender, purple
Leptospermum laevigatum	■				White
Mahonia	■				Yellow
Melaleuca	■	■	■		Cream, pink
Nerium oleander	■	■	■		Various
Plumbago auriculata	■	■	■		Blue
Potentilla fruticosa	■	■			Various
Punica granatum	■	■			Cream, orange red
Pyracantha	■				White
Rhaphiolepis indica	■			■	White, pink
Rosa	■	■	■		Various
Rosmarinus officinalis	■			■	Blue
Salvia	■	■	■		Various
Tecoma stans	■	■	■		Yellow
Vines					
Bougainvillea	■	■			Various
Campsis radicans		■			Yellow, orange red
Distictis buccinatoria	■	■	■		Red

Distictis buccinatoria

Papaver orientale

NAME OF PLANT	SPRING	SUMMER	FALL	WINTER	FLOWER COLORS
Vines (cont'd)					
Lonicera japonica 'Halliana'	■	■			Yellow
Macfadyena unguis-cati	■				Yellow
Solandra maxima	■			■	Yellow
Sollya heterophylla		■			Blue
Tecomaria capensis			■	■	Yellow, orange
Wisteria	■				Lavender, white, pink
Perennials					
Achillea	■	■			White, red, pink, yellow
Agapanthus orientalis		■			White, blue
Aloe arborescens			■		Red
Arctotis	■	■			Various
Armeria maritima	■				White, pink, red
Asclepias tuberosa		■			Orange
Baptisia australis		■			Blue
Centranthus ruber	■	■			White, pink, red
Cerastium tomentosum		■			White
Convolvulus mauritanicus		■	■		Blue
Coreopsis		■	■		Yellow
Dietes vegeta	■	■	■		White
Echinacea purpurea		■			White, red, purple
Echinops exaltatus		■	■		Blue
Echium fastuosum	■				Blue
Erigeron karvinskianus	■	■			White pink

NAME OF PLANT	SPRING	SUMMER	FALL	WINTER	FLOWER COLORS
Perennials (cont'd)					
Eryngium amethystinum		■			Blue
Euryops pectinatus	■	■	■		Yellow
Gaillardia grandiflora		■	■		Various
Gaura lindheimeri	■	■	■		White pink
Gazania	■	■			Various
Helenium autumnale		■	■		Various
Helianthemum nummularium	■	■			Various
Helianthus salicifolius		■	■		Yellow
Helleborus	■			■	Light green
Iris	■				Various
Kniphofia uvaria	■	■			Various
Liatris spicata		■			White, violet
Limonium		■			White, pink, purple
Linum	■	■			Blue
Lobelia laxiflora		■			Orange red
Mirabilis jalapa		■	■		Various
Oenothera	■	■			Pink, yellow
Osteospermum fruticosum	■		■	■	White, purple
Papaver orientale	■				Various
Penstemon	■	■			Various
Perovskia atriplicifolia		■			Blue
Romneya coulteri	■	■			White
Rudbeckia hirta		■			Various
Sedum	■	■			Various
Verbena rigida		■	■		Lavender, purple

Patio & Shade Trees

Moderate size, a minimum of litter, and limited water needs make these trees good choices for a patio or small garden.

Parkinsonia aculeata

Lagerstroemia indica

NAME OF PLANT	EVERGREEN	DECIDUOUS	FLOWER COLORS
Acacia baileyana	■		Yellow
Acer ginnala		■	
Acer negundo 'Variegatum'		■	
Acer nigrum		■	
Brachychiton populneus	■		Off-white
Callistemon citrinus	■		Red
Casuarina stricta	■		
Catalpa speciosa		■	White
Cedrus	■		
Celtis		■	
Ceratonia siliqua	■		
Cercidium floridum		■	Yellow
Chilopsis linearis		■	White, pink
Chitalpa		■	Pink
Chorisia speciosa		■	Pink, red
Eriobotrya japonica	■		White
Eucalyptus (some)	■		Cream, pink, red
Ficus carica		■	
Fraxinus velutina		■	
Geijera parviflora	■		

NAME OF PLANT	EVERGREEN	DECIDUOUS	FLOWER COLORS
Ginkgo biloba		■	
Gleditsia triacanthos		■	
Grevillea robusta	■		Orange
Jacaranda mimosifolia		■	White, lavender
Juglans hindsii		■	
Koelreuteria paniculata		■	Yellow
Lagerstroemia indica		■	White, pink, purple
Lyonothamnus floribundus asplenifolius	■		White
Melaleuca	■		White, pink
Melia azedarach		■	White
Metrosideros excelsus	■		Red
Olea europaea	■		
Parkinsonia aculeata		■	Yellow
Pistacia chinensis		■	
Prosopis glandulosa		■	Yellow
Quercus	■	■	
Rhus lancea	■		
Robinia		■	White, pink
Sophora secundiflora	■		Violet blue
Tristania conferta	■		Yellow
Ziziphus jujuba		■	Yellow

Shaded Gardens

A reduced amount of light, along with lower temperatures, characterizes garden areas shaded by trees or structures. Here are a number of plants that prefer shaded gardens or tolerate partial shade.

Hypericum calycinum

Aucuba japonica

Escallonia

Lonicera japonica 'Halliana'

NAME OF PLANT	FOLIAGE	TYPE OF PLANT	FLOWER COLORS
Acanthus mollis	E	Perennial	White, pink
Agapanthus	E	Perennial	White, blue
Arbutus unedo	E	Shrub	White
Asparagus densiflorus	E	Perennial	
Aucuba japonica	E	Shrub	
Carissa macrocarpa	E	Shrub	White
Centranthus ruber	E	Perennial	White, pink, red
Chamaerops humilis	E	Palm	
Coprosma kirkii	E	Ground cover	
Distictis buccinatoria	E	Vine	Red
Erigeron karvinskianus	E	Perennial	White, pink
Escallonia	E	Shrub	White, pink, red
Garrya elliptica	E	Shrub	Greenish yellow
Helleborus	E	Perennial	Light green
Heteromeles arbutifolia	E	Shrub	White
Hypericum calycinum	E	Ground cover	Yellow
Juniperus	E	Shrub, ground cover	
Laurus nobilis	E	Shrub	
Lonicera japonica 'Halliana'	E	Vine	Yellow
Mahonia	E	Shrub	Yellow

NAME OF PLANT	FOLIAGE	TYPE OF PLANT	FLOWER COLORS
Myrsine africana	E	Shrub	
Nandina domestica	E	Shrub	White
Ochna serrulata	E	Shrub	Yellow
Osmanthus	E	Shrub	
Phormium tenax	E	Perennial	
Pittosporum tobira	E	Shrub	White
Rhamnus	E, D	Shrub	
Rhaphiolepis indica	E	Shrub	White, pink
Ribes viburnifolium	E	Ground cover	
Sedum	E	Perennial, ground cover	Various
Solanum jasminoides	E	Vine	White
Sollya heterophylla	E	Vine-shrub	Blue
Symphoricarpos	D	Shrub	
Taxus baccata	E	Shrub	
Tecomaria capensis	E	Vine-shrub	Orange red
Thymus	E	Perennial, ground cover	White, pink
Wisteria	D	Vine	White, lavender, pink
Xylosma congestum	E	Shrub	

E = Evergreen, D = Deciduous

Plants for Hillsides

Hillsides offer a challenging set of conditions for plant growth, including shallow soil, water runoff, and dryness from sun and wind. Once established, these plants will cope well with unfavorable hillside conditions and infrequent watering.

Cerastium tomentosum (white) & Limonium perezii (purple)

Cistus purpureus

NAME OF PLANT	FOLIAGE	TYPE OF PLANT	FLOWERS	EROSION CONTROL
Acacia	E	Tree, shrub	■	■
Agave	E	Perennial		
Ailanthus altissima	D	Tree		■
Arctostaphylos	E	Shrub, ground cover	■	
Atriplex	D, E	Shrub		
Baccharis pilularis	E	Ground cover		
Bougainvillea	E	Vine	■	
Campsis radicans	D	Vine	■	
Carissa macrocarpa	E	Shrub, ground cover	■	
Ceanothus	E	Shrub, ground cover	■	■
Centranthus ruber	E	Perennial	■	
Cerastium tomentosum	E	Ground cover	■	
Cercis occidentalis	D	Shrub	■	
Cistus	E	Shrub, ground cover	■	■
Convolvulus cneorum	E	Shrub	■	
Convolvulus mauritanicus	E	Ground cover	■	
Coprosma kirkii	E	Ground cover		■
Cotoneaster	E, D	Shrub, ground cover	■	■
Cytisus	E	Shrub	■	
Echium fastuosum	E	Perennial	■	
Elaeagnus	E, D	Tree, shrub		
Eriogonum	E	Shrub	■	
Fremontodendron	E	Shrub	■	
Genista	D	Shrub	■	
Heteromeles arbutifolia	E	Shrub	■	
Hypericum calycinum	E	Ground cover	■	■
Juniperus	E	Shrub, ground cover		■
Lantana	E	Shrub, ground cover	■	■
Lonicera japonica 'Halliana'	E	Vine	■	■
Mahonia repens	E	Ground cover	■	■
Myoporum parvifolium	E	Ground cover	■	
Oenothera berlandieri	E	Perennial	■	
Osteospermum fruticosum	E	Ground cover	■	■
Plumbago auriculata	E	Shrub	■	
Pyracantha	E	Shrub	■	
Ribes viburnifolium	E	Ground cover		■
Romneya coulteri	E	Perennial	■	■
Rosa rugosa	D	Shrub	■	■
Rosmarinus officinalis	E	Shrub	■	■
Salvia	E	Shrub, perennial	■	
Santolina	E	Shrub	■	
Sollya heterophylla	E	Vine-shrub	■	
Sophora secundiflora	E	Shrub	■	
Taxus baccata 'Repandens'	E	Shrub		
Tecomaria capensis	E	Vine	■	
Teucrium fruticans	E	Shrub	■	
Westringia rosmariniformis	E	Shrub	■	
Xylosma congestum	E	Shrub		

E = Evergreen, D = Deciduous

Ground Covers

Some landscape situations call for a water-thrifty ground cover that is neat and unobtrusive; other garden areas need a plant that will control erosion or perk up the site with a seasonal carpet of bright color. Some of these unthirsty plants are as ground-hugging as grass; others will grow to a mass up to about 3 feet high.

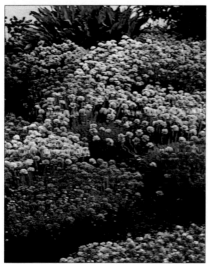

Armeria maritima

Arctostaphylos uva-ursi

NAME OF PLANT	FOLIAGE	TYPE OF PLANT	FLOWER COLORS	EROSION CONTROL
Acacia redolens	E	Shrub	Yellow	■
Aptenia cordifolia	E	Perennial	Red	
Arctostaphylos	E	Shrub	White, pink	
Armeria maritima	E	Perennial	White, pink, red	
Baccharis pilularis	E	Shrub		
Bougainvillea	E	Vine	Various	
Carissa macrocarpa	E	Shrub	White	
Ceanothus (some)	E	Shrub	Blue	
Cerastium tomentosum	E	Perennial	White	
Cistus salviifolius	E	Shrub	White	■
Convolvulus mauritanicus	E	Perennial	White	
Coprosma kirkii	E	Shrub		■
Cotoneaster horizontalis	D	Shrub	White	
Cotoneaster microphyllus	E	Shrub	White	■
Erigeron karvinskianus	E	Perennial	White, pink	
Gazania	E	Perennial	Various	
Genista	D	Shrub	Yellow	■
Juniperus (many)	E	Shrub		■
Lantana (many)	E	Shrub	Various	■

NAME OF PLANT	FOLIAGE	TYPE OF PLANT	FLOWER COLORS	EROSION CONTROL
Lonicera japonica 'Halliana'	E	Vine	Yellow	■
Mahonia (some)	E	Shrub	Yellow	■
Myoporum parvifolium	E	Shrub	White	
Nandina domestica 'Harbour Dwarf'	E	Shrub		
Osteospermum fruticosum	E	Perennial	White, purple	■
Phyla nodiflora	E	Perennial	Pink	
Ribes viburnifolium	E	Shrub		■
Rosmarinus officinalis (some)	E	Shrub	Blue	■
Santolina	E	Shrub	Yellow	
Sedum (some)	E	Perennial	White, pink, red, yellow	
Sollya heterophylla	E	Vine-shrub	Blue	
Taxus baccata 'Repandens'	E	Shrub		
Teucrium chamaedrys	E	Shrub	Blue	
Verbena rigida	E	Perennial	Lavender, purple	

E = Evergreen, D = Deciduous

Screens & Backgrounds

Look to these shrubs if you need to define a boundary, screen an unattractive feature, moderate the wind, or provide a handsome backdrop for other plants in your garden. All offer dense growth and attractive foliage.

Fremontodendron californicum

Nerium oleander

NAME OF PLANT	FOLIAGE	FLOWER COLORS	WIND CONTROL	FAST GROWING
Arbutus unedo	E	White		
Callistemon citrinus	E	Red	■	■
Calocedrus decurrens	E		■	
Caragana arborescens	D	Yellow	■	■
Carissa macrocarpa	E	White		
Ceratonia siliqua	E			
Cotoneaster lacteus	E	White		
Cupressus glabra	E		■	■
Dodonaea viscosa	E		■	
Elaeagnus	E, D		■	
Escallonia	E	White, pink, red	■	
Feijoa sellowiana	E	White, red		
Fremontodendron	E	Yellow		■
Garrya elliptica	E	Greenish yellow		
Grevillea robusta	E	Orange		■
Heteromeles arbutifolia	E	White		
Juniperus	E		■	
Laurus nobilis	E		■	

NAME OF PLANT	FOLIAGE	FLOWER COLORS	WIND CONTROL	FAST GROWING
Leptospermum laevigatum	E	White	■	
Maclura pomifera	D		■	■
Melaleuca nesophila	E	Pinkish white	■	■
Myrsine africana	E			
Nandina domestica	E	White		
Nerium oleander	E	White, pink, red, yellow	■	■
Olea europaea	E			
Osmanthus	E			
Pittosporum tobira	E	White	■	
Prunus	E	White	■	
Pyracantha	E	White	■	■
Rhamnus	E, D		■	■
Rhaphiolepis indica	E	White, pink		
Rhus lancea, R. ovata	E			
Taxus baccata	E		■	
Teucrium fruticans	E	Blue		
Westringia rosmariniformis	E	White		
Xylosma congestum	E			

E = Evergreen, D = Deciduous

The Lawn for Your Climate

In a truly water-conserving garden, no lawn is appropriate: a lawn uses up to four times more water than any other kind of planting. But by limiting the size of your lawn and selecting a turfgrass compatible with your waterwise goals, you can substantially *reduce* water consumption.

The key question in deciding whether or not to have a lawn is "Will it be used?" You may want a grassy area for children's play or for family games such as volleyball and croquet. If you need such a lawn, scale it down to the smallest feasible size and then choose an appropriate turf.

The map below shows seven regions, each possessing distinct climate conditions. For each region we list the best low-water-use lawn grasses. For information specific to your area, check with your County Cooperative Extension Office. To learn about the various grasses, consult the *Sunset* book *Lawns & Ground Covers*.

■ *Region 1:* Cool and humid, plentiful rain except in summer. Throughout this region, the grass that survives best with limited irrigation and rainfall is tall fescue. In California, Bermuda also grows well with little water.

■ *Region 2:* High temperatures, scant rainfall, dry soils. The hardy grasses—fescues, bluegrasses, and bents—need too much water here. Best choices are Bermuda, zoysia, and St. Augustine.

■ *Region 3:* Dry, semiarid climate, wide temperature fluctuations. Drought-tolerant native grasses do well: buffalo grass, crested wheatgrass, blue grama. Bluegrasses and fescues need much more water than the region's limited rainfall can provide.

■ *Region 4:* Hot, humid summers and cold, snowy winters; abundant rainfall, acid soils. If low rainfall prevails to the point where grass must be replaced, use tall fescue.

■ *Region 5:* Warm, humid, rainy summers, generally mild winters (with periodic severe ones). If low rainfall prevails to the point where grass must be replaced, use Bermuda or zoysia.

■ *Region 6:* Warm, humid, rainy summers, mild winters. If low rainfall prevails to the point where grass must be replaced, use Bermuda, tall fescue, centipede, or zoysia.

■ *Region 7:* Semitropical to tropical climate with high rainfall and year-round growing season. Adapted grasses are Bahia, Bermuda, centipede, St. Augustine, and zoysia.

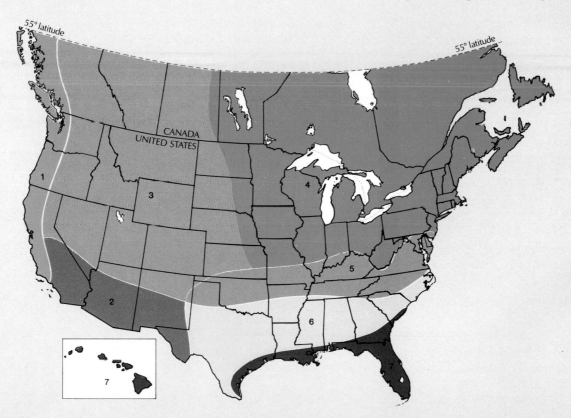

Plants for a Water-thrifty Landscape

The following plant list represents an attempt to do justice to all the regions of our country. It is weighted toward the West and Southwest because those are the regions of annual, predictable summer dry season.

Plant climate adaptability is based on minimum temperatures for plant survival. Figures are derived from plant climate maps prepared by the U.S. Department of Agriculture and by *Sunset Magazine,* supplemented by direct observations made by nursery personnel, landscape architects, and devoted gardeners. Plants are not guaranteed to survive the low temperatures mentioned here; too many intangibles are involved, including the duration and frequency of the low readings, the age and condition of the plants involved, climatic factors, and the microclimates present in every garden.

The ability to withstand freezing is not the only test of a plan's desirability in a given climate. Where other factors are especially important, we have tried to point them out.

Lack of space has kept some categories of plants out of the following lists. Bulbs, for instance, by their very nature are water thrifty; they simply close down when dry or cold weather comes and wait for better times. Many spring blooming bulbs are ideal subjects for waterwise gardens. Annuals, drought tolerant or not, do not require a long-term commitment of space. You can use them or not as the fluctuating availability of water permits.

A final word of caution: Do not remove a long-established favorite tree or shrub simply because it does not appear on the following list. Its age indicates that the plant is deeply rooted and has done well through wet years and dry; its replacement, no matter what its ultimate drought resistance may be, will need a lot of water to get started.

Versatile, undemanding gazanias provide color over several months while requiring only sunshine and a modicum of water. Use them as colorful accents— border plantings, small-scale ground cover, on hillsides, or in containers.

ACACIA. Evergreen or deciduous shrubs or trees. Native to warmer regions of the world, including the American Southwest. Leaves of many are finely divided into numerous tiny leaflets; other species have coarse foliage consisting of flattened leaf stalks that assume the function of leaves. Flowers are tiny, fluffy, creamy to bright yellow balls, often profuse enough to be showy, fragrant in some species. Tough, undemanding plants with few pests. Highly drought tolerant but need reasonably good drainage; chlorosis is a problem with water of poor quality, high soil salt content.

Acacia baileyana

Hardiness varies; many species offered in the Southwest, including California, fewer east and south. Check with local sources for new introductions. Here are a few of the 1100 species:

A. baileyana. BAILEY ACACIA. Tree grows to 20–30 ft. with feathery, blue-gray foliage and masses of fragrant yellow flowers in winter or early spring. Hardy throughout low-elevation California, borderline plant in the coastal Northwest. Not planted eastward.

A. constricta. WHITETHORN or MESCAT ACACIA. Open thorny shrub or small tree grows to 18–20 ft. with feathery foliage and fragrant yellow summer flowers. Useful in desert or low rainfall areas; can withstand temperatures to 0°F.

A. farnesiana. SWEET ACACIA. Deciduous thorny tree grows to 20 ft. with finely cut foliage and deep yellow, highly fragrant flower puffs through most of year. Attractive in frost-free climates. In colder regions, plant sold under this name is *A. minuta*, sometimes sold as *A. smallii*.

A. minuta (*A. smallii*). Resembles *A. farnesiana* but blooms in spring, and is hardy in low-elevation California and the low and intermediate deserts of Arizona.

A. redolens (sometimes sold as *A. ongerup*). Evergreen ground cover shrub to 2 ft. tall, 15 ft. wide. Has broad, dark gray green leaves (actually flattened leaf stalks). Yellow puffs in spring. Hardiness same as for *A. minuta*.

A. schaffneri. Resembles *A. minuta*, but with curving branches like tentacles. Fragrant spring bloom.

ACANTHUS mollis. Evergreen or deciduous perennial; plant possesses strong architectural lines. Stately, spreading plant with large (to 2 ft. long), deeply cut leaves springing from creeping underground rhizomes. Rigid spikes of white and purplish rose flowers 3–4 ft. tall in spring or early summer. Prefers shade but will take sun in cool-summer areas.

Acanthus mollis

In mild winter climates plant will go dormant without some summer water. Dormant in winter where freezing weather is common; mulch to protect roots. Plant withstands much neglect, but roots can be hard to eradicate.

ACER. MAPLE. Deciduous trees (rarely large shrubs). Few can withstand true prolonged drought without supplementary irrigation, but some require less water than the majority.

A. ginnala. AMUR MAPLE. Shrub or small (to 20 ft.) tree with 3-lobed leaves, ornamental clusters of red winged fruits, and brilliant scarlet fall color. Hardy to −30°F.

A. glabrum. ROCKY MOUNTAIN MAPLE. Multi-trunked shrub to 6 ft. or a 30-ft. tree. Its 2- to 5-in. leaves, lobed or divided into leaflets, turn yellow in the fall. Useful in its native Rocky Mountain region.

A. negundo. BOX ELDER. Fast growing tree (to 60 ft.) flourishes anywhere, but recommended only where conditions are too difficult for other trees. Leaves divided into 3 to 9 leaflets; fall color is yellow. Roots are aggressive, wood is weak, and tree seeds itself prolifically. Attractive *A. n.* 'Variegatum' has leaves edged creamy white and is less rambunctious than the species. Protect tree from hottest sun.

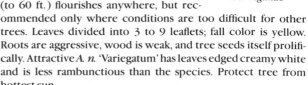

Acer negundo

A. saccharum. SUGAR MAPLE. Large shade tree noted for splendid yellow, orange, or red fall color. Not drought-resistant in any common sense of the word. *A. s. grandidentatum,* BIGTOOTH or WASATCH MAPLE, can reach 40 ft., has sharp-toothed, lobed leaves to 5 in. across and fine fall color. Conservative water user in the Rocky Mountain area. *A. s. nigrum* (*A. nigrum*). BLACK MAPLE. Resembles sugar maple but tolerates more heat and needs less water. Hardy to −40°F.

ACHILLEA. YARROW. Perennials. Most have finely divided, fernlike leaves and clustered flowers resembling small daisies. Lower-growing kinds useful as ground cover or in rock gardens; taller varieties used as border perennials. Need sun; can endure poor soil and considerable drought once established. Divide when clumps become crowded. Hardy anywhere.

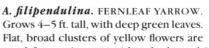

A. filipendulina. FERNLEAF YARROW. Grows 4–5 ft. tall, with deep green leaves. Flat, broad clusters of yellow flowers are good for cutting; use either fresh or dried. 'Gold Plate' and 'Coronation Gold' are more compact growers.

Achillea filipendulina

A. millefolium. COMMON YARROW. Erect growth to 3 ft. or spreading (especially if mowed; it can become a lawn weed), with dark green fernlike leaves and flat clusters of white flowers. Garden varieties include 'Rosea' (pink flowers) and 'Fire King' (red flowers). Recent hybrids have flowers in shades of pink, salmon, pale yellow, and red.

A. taygetea. Upright habit to 1½ ft. Gray green leaves. Bright yellow flowers fading to primrose.

A. tomentosa. WOOLLY YARROW. Flat, spreading mat of furry, ferny, deep green leaves topped by 6- to 10-in. stems with yellow, pale yellow, or cream flowers. Use as edging or ground cover.

AESCULUS californica. CALIFORNIA BUCKEYE. Big shrub or spreading, multi-trunked tree to 20 ft. or more. Leaves divided fanwise into 5–7 rich green 3- to 6-in. leaflets. Tall clusters of creamy flowers stand up like candles on branch ends

Aesculus californica

in spring. Leathery capsules containing big, shiny brown nuts follow; nuts are inedible.

Can endure long summer drought, but loses leaves in early summer without water. Leaves remain until fall with minimal summer watering. Trunk and branch pattern is picturesque. Hardy to near 0°F.

AGAPANTHUS. LILY-OF-THE-NILE. Perennial with thick rootstocks, heavy roots for water storage, clumps of broad, strapshaped leaves. Flowers (usually blue, white in some varieties) are in dense, round clusters atop long stems. All are water-loving by nature but can tolerate much drought when well established. Hardy to about 10°F. Where winters are colder, grow plants in tubs or large pots and protect over winter.

Agapanthus orientalis

A. Headbourne Hybrids. Deciduous, but hardier than *A. orientalis* (to 0°F., lower with heavy mulching).

A. orientalis. Large clumps of evergreen leaves produce 4- to 5-ft. stems with up to 100 flowers on each.

AGAVE. Rosettes of thick, fleshy leaves ranging from 1 ft. to 10 ft. or more across. Leaves usually spine-tipped with fierce thorns along edges. When mature (much less than a century) plants send up a gigantic flowering stalk, then die. (Most leave offsets behind to carry on.)

Agave americana

Most are true desert plants that can endure severe drought, but they can endure garden water as well. Most can take occasional temperature dips into the low teens.

A. americana. CENTURY PLANT. Blue green leaves (striped yellow or white in some varieties) grow to 6 ft. long with hooked spines along edges and a long, stiff, needlelike spine at the tip. Eventually produces a tall (15–40 ft.) inflorescence. Make sure you have room for this one—and determination enough to remove it once the flowering rosette and stem die.

A. parryi huachucensis. Broad, gray green leaves with black spines curve inward to produce a rosette like a 2- to 3-ft.-wide artichoke.

AILANTHUS altissima. TREE-OF-HEAVEN. Deciduous tree grows rapidly to 50 ft. Leaves 1–3 ft. long with 13–25 leaflets 3- to 5-in. long. Inconspicuous flowers are followed by large clusters of reddish brown, winged fruits. Foliage is smelly when crushed, tree spreads aggressively by suckers and seedlings. Not much admired and seldom planted, it often appears spontaneously, bringing a tropical look to waste places, especially in cities. Endures drought, heat, cold, poor soil, smog, soot, and dust. Hardy anywhere except very coldest climates.

Ailanthus altissima

ALOE. Succulent herbs, shrubs, rarely small trees. All make rosettes of fleshy leaves and produce simple or branched clus-

ters of red, orange, yellow, or creamy flowers. Scores of species exist, but only a few are generally available. Once established they need little water beyond rainfall to survive, but look better with occasional irrigation. Smaller kinds are useful ground cover, while larger species serve as shrubs or garden decoration. Most are hardy to around 25°F.; some withstand an occasional dip to the high teens. Not fussy about soil. Need good drainage.

Aloe arborescens

A. arborescens. TREE ALOE. Makes massive clumps to 18 ft. high and as wide, with heavy, spiky red (occasionally yellow) flower clusters in winter. Can take sun or shade, salt winds near the ocean.

A. saponaria. Short stemmed clumps of 8-in.-wide leaves, deep green liberally marked with paler spots, multiply freely to make a coarse, showy ground cover. Branched clusters of orange red to shrimp pink flowers appear in spring and last a long time.

ALYOGYNE huegelii. BLUE HIBISCUS. Evergreen shrub. Grows to 5–8 ft., with deeply lobed, rough-textured leaves. Flowers 4 to 5 in. across bloom nearly year round. Colors range from pale to intense lilac blue; buy in bloom, or look for named selections. Needs full sun, good drainage. Hardy to about 23°F., but extended or repeated frost will kill it.

Alyogyne huegelii

ANTENNARIA rosea. PUSSY TOES. Perennial rock garden plant or small-space ground cover. Makes an evergreen mat of 1-in. gray green leaves with stalks 8–12 in. tall topped by clustered flower heads of dusty rose. Native to the mountains of western North America. Hardy well below 0°F.

Antennaria rosea

APTENIA cordifolia (Mesembryanthemum cordifolium). Shrubby trailing perennial used as a ground cover. Fleshy, heart-shaped, 1-in. bright green leaves set off inch-wide red flowers in spring and summer. Color and density of foliage make it useful in sunny, dry regions where frost is rare. The plant sold as 'Red Apple', a hybrid between *Aptenia* and a related ice plant, is considered to be more vigorous.

Aptenia cordifolia

ARBUTUS unedo. STRAWBERRY TREE. Evergreen big shrub or small tree; slow growing to 8–35 ft. Bark is rich red brown, with older, dark brown bark peeling off. Trunk and limbs become picturesque and gnarled with age. Leaves are dark green, 2–3 in. long, on red stalks. Clusters of small white urn-shaped flowers appear in fall and winter, at the same time that fruit set the previous year is turning from yel-

Arbutus unedo

low and orange to red. Strawberrylike in appearance and texture, the ¾-in. fruits are mealy and insipid, though edible.

Hardy to occasional temperature drops to near 0°F., strawberry tree can tolerate a wide range of well drained soils, much or little water, ocean wind, desert heat (with partial shade). Prune it into an attractive small tree or let it grow naturally as a dense screen. 'Compacta' is a smaller, more compact plant.

ARCTOSTAPHYLOS. MANZANITA. Evergreen shrubs ranging from creepers to small tree size. Most have shiny, leathery leaves and crooked, picturesque branches with red to red brown or nearly black smooth or flaking stems. Clusters of small, urn-shaped, white or pink flowers bloom in late winter or spring. Most varieties are native to the western United States; one grows over most of northern America and Eurasia. All require good drainage; most can take extended dry periods once they are established.

Arctostaphylos densiflora

Pacific coast species and selections from them are numerous; most are low or trailing shrubs with branches that root when in contact with soil. All these demand excellent drainage and occasional water until established. Many cannot tolerate much summer water, which limits their use over much of the country. Here are a few of the best and easiest:

A. densiflora 'Howard McMinn'. Dense, spreading growth to 5–6 ft. (usually less) tall and 7 ft. wide. Leaves to 1 in. long; flowers pinkish to white in late winter. Plant takes shearing well and can be used as a hedge or tall ground or bank cover. Hardy to 10°F.

A. 'Emerald Carpet'. Dense carpet 9–14 in. tall, with bright green ½-in. leaves and inconspicuous pink flowers. Tolerant of summer water, needs it every 2–3 weeks where summers are hot and rainless. Hardy to 10°F.

A. uva-ursi. BEARBERRY, KINNIKINNICK. Prostrate grower spreads gradually to 15 ft., with 1-in. leaves, white or pinkish flowers, pink to red fruit. Excellent ground cover, except in desert climates or where soil is alkaline. Native to northern North America and Eurasia. Buy plants propagated from selected named forms for uniformity and hardiness. Some are hardy well below 0°F.

ARCTOTIS. AFRICAN DAISY. Annuals or perennials. Spreading plants 1–1½ ft. tall, with lobed leaves and large daisylike flower heads in shades of white, pink, red, purple, yellow, and orange, often with dark rings around the dark eye spot; selected colors may be rooted from cuttings. Leaves are gray green and lobed. Kinds usually seen are hybrids grown from seed. In mild-winter climates, they grow in winter, bloom

Arctotis

in spring and summer, then rebloom in fall and early winter. Need water while making growth, but survive on very little thereafter, even in sand dunes.

Plants may survive as perennials in mild climates, but first-year bloom is best. Grow as annuals where winters are cold. Hardy to moderate frost.

ARMERIA maritima. THRIFT, SEA PINK. Evergreen perennials used as ground cover, rock garden plants, edging, filler between paving blocks. Tufts of foliage resemble grass clumps. Clusters of small pink (rarely white) flowers top 6- to 10-in. stalks in spring (nearly all year on Pacific Coast). Needs excellent drainage. Spreads slowly to form a solid flowering mat. Hardy to 0°F. or below.

Armeria maritima

ARTEMISIA. Shrubs or shrubby aromatic perennials. Most grown for attractive gray or silvery foliage; a few are herbs. Flowers inconspicuous. Plants do not need rich soil but must have adequate drainage. Most are hardy to well below 0°F.

A. absinthium. COMMON WORMWOOD. Evergreen woody-based perennial 2–4 ft. tall, with finely divided silver gray leaves; these have a strong aromatic odor when bruised. Yellow flowers are insignificant. Pinch and prune to control form; divide and replant every 3–5 years to maintain vigor. Gray foliage attractive with bright flower colors. 'Lambrook Silver' is a choice selection.

Artemisia absinthium

A. caucasica. SILVER SPREADER. Spreading mat 3–6 in. tall. Finely cut, silky, silvery leaves. Inconspicuous yellowish flowers. Hardy to extreme heat and cold; fire retardant.

A. schmidtiana. ANGEL'S HAIR. Mound of finely cut, silvery, woolly white foliage to 2 ft. tall and 1 ft. wide. Variety 'Silver Mound' grows only 1 ft. tall. Both kinds are useful for foliage color contrast.

A. tridentata. BIG SAGEBRUSH. Common native of intermountain West. Grows 1½–15 ft. tall with tiny, gray green leaves. Not often planted, but can be pruned into a picturesque shrub in regions where it is native.

ASCLEPIAS tuberosa. BUTTERFLY WEED. Perennial roots send up 3-ft. stems topped by flattish clusters of brilliant orange flowers in summer. This milkweed attracts butterflies. Variations from yellow to red may be raised from seed (chill seed first). Likes full sun, good drainage, little summer water.

Asclepias tuberosa

ASPARAGUS densiflorus (often sold as *A. d.* 'Sprengeri' or *A. d.* 'Myers'). SPRENGER ASPARAGUS, MYERS ASPARAGUS. Perennials with tuberous roots, closely branched stems, feathery foliage.

Sprenger asparagus has arching or trailing stems with bundles of 1-in. leaves (actually leaflike branches), tiny white flowers, and bright red berries. Hardy to 24°F. Plant may be used as a ground cover; it's also useful as a house plant (needs bright light) or hanging basket plant. Outdoors, plant looks best in light shade with water, but tuberous roots tide it over dry periods.

Asparagus densiflorus 'Sprengeri'

Myers asparagus has erect stems and is more densely foliaged; plant looks like a cluster of upright green foxtails. Slightly less hardy than Sprenger asparagus.

ATRIPLEX. SALTBUSH. Evergreen or deciduous shrubs useful for tolerance of alkaline soils, drought, salty ocean wind, and fire retardance. Leaves gray or silvery. Flowers and fruits are not showy but are attractive to birds.

A. canescens. FOUR-WING SALTBUSH. Evergreen to 3–6 ft. tall, 4–8 ft. wide. Narrow gray leaves ½–2 in. long. Hardiest (to 0°F. or below).

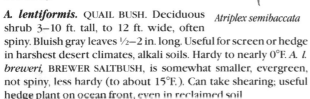

Atriplex semibaccata

A. lentiformis. QUAIL BUSH. Deciduous shrub 3–10 ft. tall, to 12 ft. wide, often spiny. Bluish gray leaves ½–2 in. long. Useful for screen or hedge in harshest desert climates, alkali soils. Hardy to nearly 0°F. *A. l. breweri,* BREWER SALTBUSH, is somewhat smaller, evergreen, not spiny, less hardy (to about 15°F.). Can take shearing; useful hedge plant on ocean front, even in reclaimed soil.

A. semibaccata. AUSTRALIAN SALTBUSH. Gray green ground cover shrub 1 ft. tall, to 6 ft. wide. Dense cover, deep rooted for erosion control, high fire retardance. Hardy to about 20°F.

AUCUBA japonica. JAPANESE AUCUBA. Evergreen shrub 6–10 ft. tall, rarely taller. Leaves are leathery, shiny, deeply toothed, 3–8 in. long, deep blackish green or variegated with yellow or white. Inconspicuous maroon flowers followed by bright red ¾-in. berries if both male and female plants are present. Needs shade and tolerates deep shade under trees or overhangs; competes successfully with tree roots. Plant will withstand some drought once it's established, but it looks better with average watering.

Aucuba japonica

Many variegated kinds are sold; best known is 'Variegata', GOLD DUST PLANT, with dark green leaves spotted with yellow. 'Picturata' ('Aureo-maculata') has yellow-centered leaves edged with dark green dotted yellow. Plain green forms are 'Longifolia' ('Salicifolia'), with narrow leaves, and 3-ft. tall 'Nana'.

BACCHARIS pilularis. COYOTE BRUSH. Evergreen shrub 8–24 in. tall, spreading to 6 ft. or more. Mounding ground cover with closely set ½-in. toothed, bright green leaves. Flowers insignificant, but female plants produce objectionable fluffy seeds that blow about; plant only cutting-grown male varieties 'Twin Peaks' or 'Pigeon Point'. The latter is taller, faster growing, and lighter green.

Baccharis pilularis

Valuable bank or ground cover for low-maintenance, low-water situations. Although a coastal California native, it has wide range of tolerance—seashore to desert, and damp soil to no water at all in cool coastal climates. Prune shrub annually to remove strongly upright branches and to thin.

BAPTISIA australis. FALSE INDIGO. Perennial 3–6 ft. tall with bluish green leaves divided into three 2½-in. leaflets. Spike-like clusters of deep blue flowers appear in early summer; trim off before inflated seed capsules appear for repeat bloom. Both flowers and seed pods are interesting in arrangements.

Thrives on ordinary garden care, but deep roots enable it to withstand long dry spells. Hardy below 0°F.

Baptisia australis

BEAUCARNEA recurvata. PONYTAIL, BOTTLE PALM. Big shrub or oddly shaped tree with enormous bulbous base (onion size in small plants, to 4 ft. across in mature plants. Plants have a single stem for years, eventually branch; stems end in tufts of long (to 3 ft.), drooping grasslike leaves to ¾ in. wide. Old plants produce clusters of tiny white flowers.

Common nearly everywhere as a house plant; hardy out of doors to 18°F. when mature; younger plants and plants in containers may freeze in the mid 20's. Needs only occasional water once established.

Beaucarnea recurvata

BOUGAINVILLEA. Evergreen shrubby vine. Although they thrive in moist tropical climates, bougainvilleas bloom better with limited summer water rations. Once established, they can endure long dry periods. Most are tall vines, but some compact forms are small enough for shrub borders or containers.

Both vining and shrubby kinds make striking ground or bank covers, with flowers (actually flower bracts) of purple, red, pink, bronze, orange, yellow, or white. Bracts of some varieties change color as they age.

Bougainvillea

Hardiest varieties, tolerating light frost, are *B. spectabilis* (*B. brasiliensis*), with purple flowers, and 'San Diego Red', with bright red flowers. Others need the protection of a warm wall or some sort of cover when frosts threaten. Take extra care in planting; root system is poorly knit and sensitive to disturbance.

BRACHYCHITON populneus. BOTTLE TREE. Evergreen tree to 30–50 ft. with 30-ft. spread. Heavy trunk, broad at base but quickly tapering, gives tree its name. Leaves are egg-shaped, tapering, to 3 in. long. They shimmer in the breeze like poplar leaves. Small creamy flowers are attractive at close range but not showy. Woody fruits can become a litter problem. Useful tree in low and intermediate deserts of Arizona, where it is used as a screen or tall, bulky windbreak. It is subject to Texas root rot. Can withstand long periods without irrigation. Hardy to about 20°F.

Brachychiton populneus

BRAHEA armata. MEXICAN BLUE PALM. Evergreen fan palm is slow growing to 40 ft., with 6- to 8-ft. spread. Broad fronds are silvery blue. White flowers bloom in long, drooping, heavy clusters. One of most heat- and drought-resistant palms. Hardy to 18°F.

Similar, but with light green leaves, is *B. edulis,* GUADALUPE PALM, a slow grower to 30 ft., with a heavily, strongly patterned trunk. Hardy below 20°F.

Brahea armata

BROUSSONETIA papyrifera. PAPER MULBERRY. Deciduous tree to an eventual 50 ft., with nearly equal spread. Bark smooth and gray; leaves rough and harsh above, pale and velvety below, 4–8 in. long, heart-shaped (often variously lobed on young growth). Tolerates heat, drought, wind, poor rocky or alkaline soil. Hardy to below 0°F.

Broussonetia papyrifera

CAESALPINIA. POINCIANA. Evergreen or deciduous shrubs or trees of fast growth. Tolerate extreme heat and thrive on infrequent, deep watering and well drained soil. Leaves are finely divided into many small leaflets. Clustered flowers notable for long, protruding, colorful stamens. Most used in desert, but can be used in other mild climates.

C. gilliesii. BIRD OF PARADISE BUSH. Grows fast to 10 ft., with angular branching; filmy foliage drops in cold weather. Clusters of yellow flowers with long (4–5 in.) red stamens appear all summer. Hardy to 10–15°F.

Caesalpinia gilliesii

C. mexicana. MEXICAN BIRD OF PARADISE. Evergreen to 10–12 ft. but can be pruned to less. Lemon yellow flowers year round except in coldest months. Hardy to about 20°F.

C. pulcherrima. DWARF POINCIANA, BARBADOS PRIDE. Deciduous shrub to 10 ft. tall; evergreen in mildest winters. Clusters of orange to red flowers with long red stamens appear throughout warm weather. Hardy to about 20°F. Recovers when frozen to the ground.

CALLIANDRA. Evergreen shrubs with finely divided foliage and fluffy flower clusters consisting principally of stamens. The following are drought resistant.

C. eriophylla. FAIRY DUSTER, FALSE MESQUITE. Airy shrub to 3 ft. tall, 3–5 ft. wide. Clusters of pink to red flowers form 1½-in. balls of fluff in earliest spring. Hardy to near 0°F.

C. tweedii. TRINIDAD FLAME BUSH. Shrub 6–8 ft. tall, equally wide., with picturesque, open branching pattern. Bright red pompon flowers cluster at ends of branches and twigs. Can be trained as espalier on wall or trellis.

Calliandra tweedii

CALLISTEMON citrinus. LEMON BOTTLEBRUSH. Evergreen large shrub or small tree. Grows naturally to bulky 10- to 12-ft. shrub, but can be trained into a 20- to 25-ft. tree. Narrow 3-in. leaves densely clothe branches; new growth is coppery, then bright green. Flower clusters resemble bright red bottlebrushes—dense spikes consisting chiefly of long, bright red stamens. Persistent woody seed capsules follow. Tolerant of wide range of soil conditions and climates. Withstands drought when established, but tolerates irrigation well. Survives 20°F., but with some damage.

Callistemon citrinus

CALOCEDRUS decurrens (*Libocedrus decurrens*). INCENSE CEDAR. Evergreen tree, narrowly cone-shaped to 75–90 ft. Rich green foliage in flat sprays has pungent fragrance in warm weather. Bark deep reddish brown. Tiny cones resemble duck's bills. If watered thoroughly when young, tree will develop deep root system, tolerate extreme drought in maturity. Excellent plant for tall screen, windbreak. Hardy well below 0°F.

Calocedrus decurrens

CALOCEPHALUS brownii. CUSHION BUSH. Evergreen shrubby perennial to 3 ft. Mounds into a dense cushion of branching, wiry stems with tiny white leaves closely pressed against them. Buttonlike yellow and white flower heads. Thrives on ocean wind. Needs fast drainage. Moderately drought tolerant. Tolerates only light frost.

Calocephalus brownii

CAMPSIS radicans (*Bignonia radicans*). Deciduous vine climbing by clinging aerial roots to 40 ft. Leaves are divided into toothed leaflets, each 2½ in. long. Clustered flowers are trumpet-shaped, deep orange tubes flaring to 2-in.-wide red faces. Rampant vine; needs occasional heavy pruning to keep it in bounds. Can spread aggressively from suckers if roots are cut or if prostrate branches are allowed to root. Variety 'Flava' has yellow flowers. Hardy to − 20°F.

Campsis radicans

C. tagliabuana. 'Mme. Galen', a hybrid between *C. radicans* and a Chinese species, is a smaller vine or sprawling shrub with salmon red flowers.

CARAGANA. PEASHRUB. Deciduous shrubs or small trees from Russia, Siberia, and Manchuria. Leaves are divided into small leaflets. Yellow sweet pea-shaped flowers in spring. Hardy to any cold; extremely tolerant of wind, drought. Useful in high plains, mountains, desert.

C. arborescens. SIBERIAN PEASHRUB. Small tree of rapid growth to 20 ft.

Caragana arborescens

C. frutex. RUSSIAN PEASHRUB. Shrubby, to 10 ft. 'Globosa' is smaller shrub of dense growth habit.

CARISSA macrocarpa. NATAL PLUM. Evergreen shrub. Mounding growth to 5–7 ft. with leathery, shiny, roundish oval leaves. Starlike, 2-in.-wide, fragrant white flowers are followed by 1- to 2-in. red edible fruit with a taste resembling a sweetish cranberry. Branches are spiny, making Natal plum a good barrier plant. Use as screen, hedge, or ground cover (dwarf forms only). Endures only light frost. Established plants endure considerable drought in humid coastal climates, but need water where summers are hot and dry.

Carissa macrocarpa

Upright growers (to 6 ft.) include 'Fancy' and 'Ruby Point'; among lower-growing kinds are 'Boxwood Beauty' (2 ft., no thorns); 'Green Carpet' (1–1½ ft.); 'Horizontalis', 'Minima', and 'Prostrata' (1½–2 ft.); 'Tomlinson' (2–2½ ft., reddish-tinged foliage, no thorns); and 'Tuttle' (2–3 ft., 3–5 ft. wide, heavy fruit producer).

CARYOPTERIS clandonensis. BLUE MIST. Deciduous shrub or shrubby perennial. Many-stemmed, mounded plant 2 ft. tall with narrow, gray green leaves and whorls of small blue flowers on the upper parts of the stems. Blooms midsummer to frost if flowering shoots are removed after bloom. Usually freezes to ground in cold winter climates; trim nearly to ground in spring (frozen or not) to maintain good form. When established will withstand drought and any degree of cold, but not desert heat and wind. *C. incana* is similar, but taller (to 3–4 ft.).

Caryopteris clandonensis

CASSIA. Evergreen shrubs with leaves divided featherwise into many leaflets and yellow flowers in elongated clusters. Very large genus with new species being introduced from time to time. Most are tropical or subtropical, and many of the drought tolerant kinds are Australian natives. Once established, they can survive long periods without water but look better with at least minimal irrigation. Following kinds are grown in the desert areas of Arizona and California.

Cassia artemisioides

C. artemisioides. FEATHERY CASSIA. Grows 3–5 ft. tall, with gray leaves divided into almost needlelike leaflets 1 in. long. Clusters of 5 to 8 sulfur yellow flowers (each ¾ in.) appear winter into spring, often continuing into summer.

C. nemophila. Similar to *C. artemisioides*, but with green foliage.

C. phyllodenia. Narrow, silvery gray leaves, yellow flowers on a 5–6 ft. shrub.

C. sturtii. Gray green shrub 3–6 ft. tall. Longer bloom period than *C. artemisioides*.

CASUARINA. BEEFWOOD, SHE-OAK, AUSTRALIAN PINE. Evergreen trees, essentially leafless but with many long, thin, jointed branches that superficially resemble pine needles. Tough, undemanding trees that take heat, drought, wind, salt breezes, wet or saline soils. Hardy to about 15°F. Useful in desert or dry-summer climates, they can be weed trees in humid subtropical areas such as Florida.

C. cunninghamiana. RIVER SHE-OAK. Dark green, fine-textured branches on a vigorous, fast growing 70-ft. tree.

C. equisetifolia. HORSETAIL TREE. Fast growth to 40–60 ft. Pendulous gray green branches.

Casuarina stricta

C. stricta. MOUNTAIN or DROOPING SHE-OAK, COAST BEEFWOOD. Fast growth to 20–35 ft. Dark green branches, abundant 1-in. cones. Can be a useful street tree. Best with occasional deep watering.

CATALPA speciosa. WESTERN CATALPA. Deciduous tree to 40–70 ft., with somewhat smaller spread. Large (to 12 in. long) leaves give a tropical look. Six-inch upright clusters of white flowers with brown markings appear in late spring or early summer, followed by long, slender seed capsules often called Indian beans (inedible). Withstands cold and extended dry spells, but cannot tolerate summer-long drought. Hardy to −30°F. or lower.

Catalpa speciosa

CEANOTHUS. WILD LILAC. Evergreen shrubs (rarely small trees) or ground cover plants. Purple, blue, lavender, or white flowers are individually tiny, but borne in showy masses in spring. All the desirable species are native to the western states and cannot tolerate either continued hard freezes or regular summer irrigation. Two can be used as single or multiple stemmed small trees : 'Ray Hartman' and *C. thyrsiflorus* will grow to 20 ft. The former has medium blue flowers; blooms on the latter range from light to dark blue.

Ceanothus gloriosus

Many medium to large shrubs are available in the West; flowers range from pale to deepest indigo. 'Concha', 'Dark Star', and 'Julia Phelps' are among the darkest blue. *C. rigidus* 'Snowball' and *C. thyrsiflorus* 'Snow Flurry' have white flowers.

Ground cover kinds range from nearly flat mats (*C. hearstiorum*) to 2- to 5-ft. mounds 15 ft. or more in width (*C. griseus horizontalis* 'Yankee Point' and others).

All need good drainage and infrequent watering; established plants (a full year in the ground) will need none, except in hottest inland climates. Keep plants away from lawn sprinklers.

Widely used ground cover kinds fairly tolerant of summer water are *C. gloriosus,* 1 to 1½ ft. tall and much wider, with spiny, glossy leaves and light blue flowers, and its varieties. Dislikes high heat.

CEDRUS. CEDAR. Evergreen cone-bearing trees. These are the true cedars, bearing needles in tufted clusters on short twigs (except on new growth, where needles are borne singly). All have deep roots and can get along with little or no summer water once established. All are hardy to 0°F. or lower. Male catkins produce large amounts of pollen.

C. atlantica. ATLAS CEDAR. Slow growth to 60 ft. or more, open and angular in youth, broad-topped and picturesque in age. Bluish green 1-in. needles. Weeping, blue gray, and golden green varieties exist.

Cedrus atlantica

C. deodara. DEODAR CEDAR. Quick growth to 80 ft., with 40-ft. spread. Branches sweep down, then up in graceful fashion; topmost growth nods. Grayish green needles. Dwarf, golden, and prostrate forms exist. Easily pruned to control size. Not adaptable to low desert conditions.

C. libani. CEDAR OF LEBANON. Eventually a picturesque, irregular, wide-spreading 80-ft. tree, but slow growing. Dense cone when young, with green needles; older trees grayish green.

CELTIS. HACKBERRY. Deciduous trees related to elm and similar in appearance, but smaller. All have virtue of deep rooting—useful in narrow planting strips or near paving. All have tiny fleshy fruits attractive to birds. All endure heat, wind, drought, alkaline soil.

C. australis. EUROPEAN HACKBERRY. Moderate growth to 40 ft. or more. Has shorter deciduous period than common hackberry (*C. occidentalis*). Native to southern Europe; hardy only to 0°–10°F.

C. occidentalis. COMMON HACKBERRY. To 50 ft. tall, equally wide, with spreading, sometimes pendulous branches. Late to leaf out. Hardy well below 0°F.

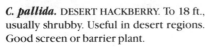

Celtis occidentalis

C. pallida. DESERT HACKBERRY. To 18 ft., usually shrubby. Useful in desert regions. Good screen or barrier plant.

C. reticulata. WESTERN HACKBERRY. To 25–30 ft.; with *C. pallida,* especially useful as ornamental tree in desert and intermountain plantings.

CENTRANTHUS ruber. JUPITER'S BEARD, RED VALERIAN. Perennial. Grows 2–3 ft. tall, with bluish green foliage and clusters of red, pink, or white flowers crowning each stem in late spring and summer. Easiest of perennials, it sows itself freely (sometimes too freely) and may need weeding out. Tolerates poor soil, hot sun or light shade, drought.

Useful and attractive where the hose won't reach—parking strips, slopes and banks, outer reaches of garden, rural roadsides. Hardy to 0°F.

Centranthus ruber

CERASTIUM tomentosum. SNOW-IN-SUMMER. Perennial. Mats of silvery white 1-in. leaves spread to 2–3 ft. Masses of white flowers ½ to ¾ in. wide rise on 6- to 8-in. stalks in early summer. Useful as edging, in rock garden, between paving elements, as small-scale ground cover.

Needs sun (lightest shade in hottest, sunniest regions), good drainage, infrequent watering. Shear after bloom. Set plants 1½ ft. apart, or sow seeds. Hardy in all climates.

Cerastium tomentosum

CERATONIA siliqua. CAROB. Evergreen tree. Left alone, it grows as a bulky multi-stemmed huge shrub; can be staked and trained into a 30–40 ft. tree. Glossy green leaves divided into nearly round 2-in. leaflets. Flowers not noticeable. Female trees produce large, flat, leathery dark brown pods (a potential clean-up problem; pods contain a sweet pulp, sometimes treated and sold as a chocolate substitute).

Avoid narrow planting sites, as roots can crack sidewalks. Water deeply and infrequently until established. Hardy to 18°F., but protect young trees against heavy freezes.

Ceratonia siliqua

CERCIDIUM floridum. BLUE PALO VERDE. Deciduous tree, fast growing to 30 ft. by 30 ft. In spring, a cloud of small, bright yellow flowers; later, an intricate pattern of bluish green spiny branches, branchlets, and leaves. Tiny leaflets fall early; leafstalks remain to give light shade. Desert favorite. Hardy to 0–10°F.

Cercidium floridum

CERCIS occidentalis. WESTERN RED-BUD. Deciduous shrub or small tree 10–18 ft. tall, usually with several trunks from the base. Blue green, roundish, 3-in. leaves turn light yellow or red in fall. Early spring flowers on bare trunk and branches are sweet pea-shaped, clustered, rich magenta, ½ in. long. Magenta seed pods follow in summer, turn to brown. Water regularly when young to speed growth. Established plants need no summer water. Hardy to 0°F.

Cercis occidentalis

CHAMAEROPS humilis. MEDITERRANEAN FAN PALM. Evergreen shrub or small tree. Rarely a single-trunk tree to 20 ft.; more commonly a clumping palm to 20 ft. and as wide. Slow growth. Leaves fan-shaped, tough, leathery, 2–3 ft. wide. Trunks rough with bases of old leaves. One of the hardiest palms (to 6°F.). Highly drought tolerant; occasional irrigation will speed growth.

Chamaerops humilis

CHILOPSIS linearis. DESERT WILLOW, DESERT CATALPA. Deciduous shrub or small tree to 25 ft. Open, airy, somewhat irregular growth habit, eventually twisted and picturesque.

Long, narrow 2- to 5-in leaves drop early. Trumpet-shaped 2-in.-long flowers of white, pink, or lavender marked with purple. Blooms when very young (first year from container). Native to southwestern deserts. Hardy to nearly 0°F.

Chilopsis linearis

CHITALPA. Deciduous tree. This recently introduced hybrid (between a catalpa and *Chilopsis*) grows into a multi-trunked 15-ft. tree in 15 years and may reach 30 ft. in time.

Bright green leaves are 1 in. wide, 4 in. long. Trumpet-shaped flowers of pink striped with purple appear continuously from spring through fall. Withstands hot winds and extended drought, but also tolerates regular watering. Can be trained into a single stemmed tree. Can be killed to the ground at 0°F., but comes back quickly from roots.

Chitalpa

CHORISIA speciosa. FLOSS SILK TREE. Nearly evergreen tree (leaves drop at fall flowering season or when temperature drops below 27°F.). Trees can reach 50–60 ft. Heavy green trunk is studded with thick, heavy spines; on older trees, spines lessen, trunk turns gray. Leaves are divided into fingerlike leaflets. Pink to red 5- to 6-in. flowers in autumn.

Needs excellent drainage, limited water. Water established trees deeply once a month. Has survived 12–15°F. with severe limb and trunk damage.

Chorisia speciosa

CISTUS. ROCKROSE. Evergreen shrubs. Profuse flowering, drought and deer resistance, fire retardance all recommend rockroses. All will grow in poor, rocky soil and can tolerate heat, wind (including ocean wind), and scanty water—no water once established. All are hardy to 15°F.

Use them as ground or bank cover, screens or dividers, or in wild areas. Spring or early summer flowers resemble single roses; foliage, smooth or crinkled, is often pleasantly aromatic.

Cistus purpureus

C. hybridus (*C. corbariensis*). WHITE ROCKROSE. Grows 2–5 ft. tall and as wide. Crinkly gray green leaves are fragrant. Flowers 1½ in. wide, white with yellow centers.

C. incanus (*C. villosus*). To 3–5 ft. tall, equally wide, with downy gray leaves and purplish pink 2-in. flowers. Highly flame retardant.

C. ladanifer. CRIMSON-SPOT ROCKROSE. From 3–5 ft. tall, compact, with dark green, fragrant, 4-in. leaves; flowers are 3 in. wide, white with a deep red spot at the base of each petal.

C. purpureus. ORCHID ROCKROSE. Compact growth to 4 ft. tall and as wide (broader, lower in constant ocean wind). Dark green 1- to 2-in. leaves, reddish purple 3-in. flowers with a deep red spot at the base of each petal. Fine choice where cool ocean winds prevail.

C. salviifolius (usually sold as *C. villosus* 'Prostratus'). SAGE-LEAF ROCKROSE. Spreading shrub to 2 ft. tall, 6 ft. wide, with gray green, crinkly looking leaves. Profuse show of 1½-in. white, yellow-centered flowers. Useful ground cover for difficult sites; tough enough for highway landscaping.

CONVOLVULUS. MORNING GLORY. Two compact species from southern Europe and North Africa have low water requirements and make excellent cover for dry banks, feature plants in large rock gardens. They prefer loose, fast draining soil and full sun. Hardy to 10–15°F.

Convolvulus cneorum

C. cneorum. BUSH MORNING GLORY. Fast growing shrub to 2–4 ft. tall and as wide. Leaves silky, silvery gray, 1–2½ in. long. White or pink morning glories with yellow throats open from pink buds May to September. Can take light shade. Prune severely to prevent legginess. Fire retardant if healthy.

C. mauritanicus. GROUND MORNING GLORY. Evergreen perennial 1–2 ft. tall with 3 ft. spread. Roundish, gray green leaves ½–1½ in. long. Lavender blue 1- to 2-in. morning glories open from June to November. Trim back in late winter to prevent woodiness.

COPROSMA kirkii. Evergreen shrub. Spreading shrub 2–3 ft. tall, often nearly prostrate, with long, straight stems extending horizontally from the base. Leaves ½–1 in. long, narrow, closely set on branches. Will take sun or partial shade. Accepts wide range of soils, wind, salt spray. Use as ground or bank cover. Hardy to about 15°F.

Coprosma kirkii

CORDIA boissieri. Evergreen shrub to 8–10 ft.; can be trained into a small tree or held to 3–5 ft. shrub. Gray green, rough-surfaced leaves to 5 in. long. White flowers 2½ in. wide with yellow throats. Clusters appear April–May and continue for a long season. Used in desert gardens; water deeply every 7–10 days in summer.

COREOPSIS. Sunflower relatives with yellow daisy flowers. All are easy to grow. Two are outstanding for long show of bright yellow flowers, tolerance of casual care, and low water requirements. Hardy well below 0°F.

Cordia boissieri

C. grandiflora. Perennial to 2 ft. or more with a 3-ft. spread. Bright yellow flowers 2½–3 in. wide, carried from spring to frost above dark green foliage clumps. Good cutting flowers. Semidouble to double varieties 'Early Sunrise' and 'Sunburst' will bloom first summer if sown early.

C. verticillata. Perennial 2½–3 ft. tall. Clumps of erect or slightly leaning stems with many whorls of finely cut, narrow leaves. Bright yellow daisies 2 in. wide appear all summer, fall. 'Moonbeam' has pale primrose yellow flowers on 2-ft. stems, 'Zagreb' bright yellow flowers on 1-ft. stems.

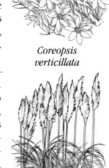

*Coreopsis
verticillata*

CORTADERIA selloana. PAMPAS GRASS. Perennial. Giant clumping grass with 8- to 10-ft. masses of narrow, arching, drooping, saw-edged leaves topped by long stalks bearing 1- to 3-ft. plumes of white to pinkish flowers. Fast growing, tough, withstands any soil or moisture condition, wind, heat, desert or coastal hazards. Evergreen to 15°F., root hardy to below 0°F. Use as windbreak, screen, bank planting, giant feature plant.

NOTE: On the West Coast, beware of a similar grass, *C. jubata*, which can become a nuisance through self-sowing. It has shorter leaves and a wider space between foliage and flower plume than *C. selloana.*

*Cortaderia
selloana*

COTINUS coggygria (Rhus cotinus). SMOKE TREE. Deciduous shrub or small tree to 25 ft., usually less. Roundish leaves 1½–3 in. long are bluish green, turning yellow to orange red in autumn. Large, loose clusters of inconspicuous flowers turn to showy smoky puffs of fuzzy fruit stalks.

'Purpureus' and 'Royal Purple' have deep purple leaves, color on the latter persisting all summer, making a striking contrast with green or gray foliage. Color best in poor or rocky soil with good drainage. Water only infrequently. Hardy well below 0°F.

Cotinus coggygria

COTONEASTER. Evergreen or deciduous shrubs, most with small leaves, profusion of tiny white or pinkish spring flowers followed by persistent red fruits for winter show. Adaptable and hardy in most climates, but low ground cover species die out in desert heat. Of many species, these are most highly recommended for drought tolerance.

*Cotoneaster
horizontalis*

C. horizontalis. ROCK COTONEASTER. Deciduous shrub out of leaf for only a short time. Grows 2–3 ft. tall, up to 15 ft. wide. Tiny roundish leaves hold late, turn orange and red before falling. Bright red berries continue show.

C. lacteus (*C. parneyi*). PARNEY COTONEASTER, RED CLUSTERBERRY. Arching growth to 6–8 ft. or more. Leathery, deep green leaves 2 in. long. Clusters of red fruit 2–3 in. in diameter last a long time. Hardy to about 0°F. Good screen plant, espalier, bank cover.

Cotoneaster lacteus

C. microphyllus. ROCKSPRAY COTONEASTER. Evergreen shrub; main branches prostrate, secondary branches to 2–3 ft., but can be shortened or removed if low ground cover is desired. Tiny (⅓-in.) dark green leaves, followed by rosy red, long-lasting fruit ¼ in. in diameter.

CUPRESSUS. CYPRESS. True cypresses come from many regions; species native to the Mediterranean and the American Southwest have low water needs.

C. arizonica (ROUGHBARK ARIZONA CYPRESS) and **C. glabra** (SMOOTH ARIZONA CYPRESS). Two similar trees from Arizona and other southwestern states. Principal difference is bark; smooth Arizona cypress sheds bark annually, showing rich cherry red new bark underneath. Fine textured, scalelike foliage is green to gray green to silvery blue. Fast growing (to 40 ft. or more), exceedingly tolerant of heat and drought. For uniformity in screen plantings, select carefully or buy named varieties propagated by cuttings. Hardy to near 0°F.

Cupressus glabra

C. sempervirens. ITALIAN CYPRESS. True species with horizontal branching is rarely seen. Most common are the varieties 'Stricta' ('Fastigiata'), COLUMNAR ITALIAN CYPRESS; or 'Glauca' (BLUE ITALIAN CYPRESS), columnar, narrow trees eventually growing to 60 ft. 'Swane's Golden' has yellow new growth. All are useful for tall, narrow feature plants, screens, or for furnishing a romantic Mediterranean aspect. Have endured occasional dips to near 0°F., but grow better in warmer climates.

CYTISUS. BROOM. Showy shrubs in the pea family. Deciduous or evergreen. Tolerate seashore conditions, wind, sun, poor soil but need good drainage. Prune plants after bloom to control size and shape and to reduce production of unattractive seed pods. Many self-sow in mild climates and pose possibility of becoming weeds if not controlled.

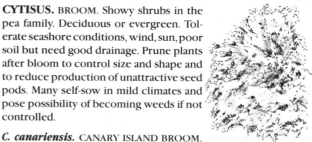

C. canariensis. CANARY ISLAND BROOM. Evergreen shrub to 6–8 ft. tall, 5–6 ft. wide with bright green leaves, clusters of bright yellow, fragrant flowers at branch ends in spring and summer. Hardy to 15°F.

Cytisus praecox

C. praecox. WARMINSTER BROOM. Deciduous, but with bright green stems for evergreen look. Grows to 3–5 ft. tall, somewhat wider. Masses of creamy white to palest yellow flowers in early spring. 'Allgold' is deeper yellow, 'Hollandia' pink. For 'Moonlight', see *C. scoparius*. Hardy to 0°F.

C. scoparius. SCOTCH BROOM. Upright masses of wandlike green stems to 10 ft. produce bright yellow flowers in spring and summer. In many regions plant has escaped from cultivation to become a weed. Named, colored varieties are smaller, less aggressive. Colors include red and white, red and yellow, lilac pink, white and purple, orange and apricot, pure white, and red. Widely grown 'Moonlight' is palest yellow, compact. Hardy to around 5–10°F.

C. spachianus (*C. racemosus, C. fragrans*). Very similar to *C. canariensis*, but with longer, looser flower clusters.

DALEA. Evergreen or deciduous shrubs or trees with finely divided leaves, clustered sweet pea-shaped flowers. Hardy to about 15–20°F.

D. greggii. TRAILING INDIGO BUSH. Useful evergreen ground cover. Prostrate; reaches 3 ft. in width in 1½ years. Pearl gray foliage, clusters of small purple flowers in spring and early summer. Takes extreme heat, drought. For fast growth, water every 2 weeks until established.

Dalea spinosa

D. spinosa. SMOKE TREE. Usually grows to 12 ft. tall, but can reach 30 ft. with summer water. Few leaves fall early. Network of gray, spiny branches resembles cloud of smoke. Fragrant violet blue flowers April–June.

DELOSPERMA. ICE PLANT. Scores of ice plants flourish in mild Mediterranean climates. All have low, creeping, and rooting habit, fleshy leaves, and many-petaled flowers that look superficially like daisies. Two are hardy enough to withstand temperatures to 0°F.:

Delosperma congestum nubigenum

D. congestum nubigenum (D. nubigenum). Bright green fleshy leaves set off scores of bright yellow, inch-wide flowers in spring. Use in rock garden or as small scale ground cover.

D. cooperi. Similar to the above, but with bright purple flowers.

DIETES vegeta (Moraea iridioides). FORTNIGHT LILY, AFRICAN IRIS. Evergreen perennial. Fan-shaped clumps of narrow, stiff, leaves can reach 4 ft.

Branching flower stalks produce a succession of waxy white 3-in. flowers with orange and brown markings, purple stippling. Each bloom lasts a day but is quickly replaced by another. Do not cut off old bloom stalks; they branch repeatedly and last from year to year. If they grow too long and fall over, cut back just above leaf joint at base of stalk. A new branch will appear and produce flowers in time. Break off seed capsules before they grow large. Heavy pods bend down flower stalks, may self-sow.

Dietes vegeta

Use as foil for rocks, gravel, bulky shrubs. Long lived, very drought tolerant. Damaged at 20°F., but will survive.

DISTICTIS buccinatoria (Bignonia cherere, Phaedranthus buccinatorius). BLOOD RED TRUMPET VINE. Evergreen vine climbing by tendrils. Leaves have two leaflets 2–4 in. long.

Clusters of 4-in. trumpet-shaped flowers open orange red with yellow throat, fading to bluish red. Bursts of flowers appear sporadically throughout the year as weather warms. Use to cover walls, fences, arbors. Water well until established. Hardy to about 20°F.

Distictis buccinatoria

DODONAEA viscosa. HOP BUSH, HOPSEED BUSH. Evergreen shrub or small tree. Green form is native to Arizona and other warm parts of the world. Fast growth to 12–15 ft. or more, with many upright stems densely clad with narrow, 4-in.-long green leaves, insignificant flowers, attractive pinkish orange winged fruits. Hardy in warmer parts of the high desert.

Dodonaea viscosa

More common is the variety 'Purpurea', with bronzy green leaves that turn deep brownish red in winter. Less hardy than green form—to about 15°F.

Both endure ordinary or poor soil, desert heat or ocean wind, drought. With little water, 6–8 ft. is a likely height. With ample water, plants grow quickly to 15 ft.

ECHINACEA purpurea (Rudbeckia purpurea). PURPLE CONEFLOWER. Perennial. Coarse, stiff clumps to 4–5 ft. Late summer and early autumn flowers are big daisies (to 6 in. across) with dark purple centers and drooping purple rays. There's also a white variety. Takes ordinary soil, full sun. Thrives on average water, but can endure long dry spells. Hardy anywhere.

Echinacea purpurea

ECHINOPS exaltatus. GLOBE THISTLE. Perennial. Rigid, erect, stiffly branching plants with deeply cut, gray green, prickly leaves. Small steel blue flowers cluster in 2-in.-thick globular heads midsummer to fall. Excellent cut flowers, fresh or dry. Takes ordinary soil, full sun. At its best with average water, but endures drought when established.

Grow from seed or divide plants in spring or fall. Use to contrast with other tough summer perennials, such as *Rudbeckia* and *Helenium.* 'Taplow Blue' is a choice variety.

Echinops exaltus

ECHIUM fastuosum. PRIDE OF MADEIRA. Shrubby perennial with mounding form, coarse branches to 6 ft. tall and wider. Hairy, elongated, gray green leaves make big tufts at end of stems. Huge spikelike clusters of blue purple form at ends of branches in late spring. Established plants can endure summer-long drought near coast, need occasional water inland. Withstands occasional light frost; severely crippled in low 20's. Spectacular plant for bank planting, large borders.

Echium fastuosum

ELAEAGNUS. Deciduous or evergreen shrubs or trees. Most are conspicuous for silvery coating of hairs or scales on leaves. Flowers are tiny, inconspicuous, often fragrant; some species have red or silvery-scaled fruit. All grow moderately fast to moderate height, making good screen or tall hedge material. All thrive on average soil, full sun, moderate water. Established plants can stand drought.

E. angustifolia. RUSSIAN OLIVE. Deciduous tree. Narrow 2-in. silvery gray leaves give it the look of true olive. Grows to 20 ft. with picturesque, often leaning, dark brown trunk and angular branches. Fragrant greenish yellow flowers precede fruit like small olives. Can withstand extremes of heat, cold, drought, but out of character in mild-winter climates.

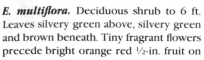

E. multiflora. Deciduous shrub to 6 ft. Leaves silvery green above, silvery green and brown beneath. Tiny fragrant flowers precede bright orange red ½-in. fruit on 1-in. stems. These are extremely acid but attractive to birds. Hardy in any but the coldest winters.

Elaeagnus pungens

E. pungens. SILVERBERRY. Evergreen shrub 4–15 ft. tall with irregular, angular growth habit easily controlled by pruning. Grayish green foliage has overall olive drab cast from rusty brown scales on leaves and twigs. Red ½-in. fruit has coating of brownish scales. Tough plant in heat and wind. Dense growth, moderate spininess make it a good barrier. Variegated kinds are lighter and brighter in effect; 'Maculata' has a gold blotch in the center of each leaf, 'Marginata' has silvery white leaf edges, and 'Variegata' has yellowish white edges. All are hardy to 0°–10°F.

ERIGERON karvinskianus. MEXICAN DAISY, SANTA BARBARA DAISY. Sprawling or trailing evergreen perennial to 10–20 in. tall, spreading wider. Rather open growth, with 1-in.-long, narrow leaves. Attractive daisies ¾ in. across are white, pink, or nearly red; all colors appear on the plant at the same time, and blossoming is nearly continuous. Self-sows and can become an attractive pest if not controlled. Average soil or poor, sun or light shade. Highly drought tolerant. Good bank cover, hanging basket plant, trailer over walls. Hardy to 15°F.

Erigeron karvinskianus

ERIOBOTRYA japonica. LOQUAT. Evergreen tree or large shrub. Grows 15–30 ft. tall, broad and bushy in full sun, more slender in partial shade. Big, glossy deep green leaves up to 1 ft. long, sharply toothed and deeply veined, give loquat a tropical look. Clusters of woolly, dull white flowers in fall; clusters of yellow to orange fruit, 1 to 2 in. long, acid to sweet. Named varieties produce best fruit.

Useful for bold foliage effect as lawn tree or espalier on wall or fence. Appreciates water, but endures drought when established; needs regular deep watering for best fruit. Safely hardy to 20°F.; has endured 12°F.

Eriobotrya japonica

ERIOGONUM. BUCKWHEAT. Shrubs or shrubby perennials. Not the grain producing buckwheat, but a group of western plants with tiny flowers in large clusters. Colors vary with species, but all age to rust or brown and are attractive over a long period. Flowers of larger kinds useful in arrangements, fresh or dried. Give sun, good drainage. Hardy to around 20°F.

E. arborescens. SANTA CRUZ ISLAND BUCKWHEAT. To 4 ft. or more and wider, with open branching and narrow gray green leaves at end of branches. Long-stalked, wide, flat clusters of pink flowers in summer.

E. giganteum. ST. CATHERINE'S LACE. Like the above, but more densely branched and with grayish white broad oval leaves 2½ in. long.

Eriogonum arborescens

ERYNGIUM amethystinum. SEA HOLLY. Perennial, with stiffly erect 2–3-ft. stems topped by clustered tiny blue flowers surrounded by a spiny ruff of blue bracts. Upper stems also blue. Flowers last long fresh or dried. Best in full sun, deep, well drained soil. Needs little water. Hardy to below 0°F.

ESCALLONIA. Evergreen shrubs with glossy, clean foliage, dense habit, and clustered small flowers in pink, red, or white. All are resistant to wind and thrive in full sun near the coast, in partial shade in hottest, driest areas. Established plants stand some drought, but are better-looking with occasional deep watering. Useful as screening, hedge, individual plant. Damaged at 10°–15°F., but usually recovers.

Eryngium amethystinum

E. bifida (E. montevidensis). WHITE ESCALLONIA. Bulky shrub to 8–10 ft.; can be trained as a multi-trunked 25-ft. tree. White flowers summer, fall.

E. 'Frades' (E. fradesii). Compact shrub to 5–6 ft., lower with pinching. Clusters of pink to rose flowers nearly all year.

E. rubra. Glossy dark green leaves set off clusters of red flowers throughout warm weather. Excellent hedge or screen plant near coast.

Escallonia rubra

EUCALYPTUS. Over 600 species of eucalyptus make generalizations difficult, but all are evergreen, nearly all are Australian, and most can endure with little water once established. Some are among the best trees for Mediterranean (summer-dry) or desert climates. They are among the fastest growing evergreens and the most pest-free (although a wood-boring beetle and a mysterious wilt have recently appeared in California). Young plants that are not root-bound in containers are best choice for planting. Unstaked plants develop strongest trunks; if you buy a spindly, staked plant, cut it back to near the ground and let it form new growth. Select the best for a permanent trunk. Soil should drain well or chlorosis (yellowing of leaves) may appear.

Eucalyptus sideroxylon

Here are a few of the hardiest among many good garden plants; flowers are white and inconspicuous unless noted:

E. camaldulensis (E. rostrata). RED GUM, RIVER RED GUM. Immense, spreading tree to 80–100 ft. or more. Branches weep gracefully. Hardy to 12°–15°F.

E. citriodora. LEMON-SCENTED GUM. Tall (75–100 ft.), slender, with white to pinkish trunk and long, narrow, lemon-scented leaves. Hardy only to 24°–28°F.

E. gunnii. CIDER GUM. Large, dense, erect 40–75 ft. tree. Hardiest large eucalypt—to 5°–10°F.

E. microtheca. COOLIBAH. Bushy, round-headed tree to 35–40 ft., with long, narrow blue green leaves. May have one or many trunks. Insignificant flowers produce tiny seed capsules, little litter. Hardy to 5°–10°F.

E. nicholii. NICHOL'S WILLOW-LEAFED PEPPERMINT. Graceful, weeping 40-ft. tree, fine-textured foliage. Fast growing. Hardy to 12°–15°F.

E. polyanthemos. SILVER DOLLAR GUM. Fast growing, 20- to 60-ft. tree with oval to round 2- to 3-in. leaves. Foliage on mature growth has lance-shaped leaves. Hardy to 14°–18°F.

E. sideroxylon. RED IRONBARK. Tree of variable size and form, 20–80 ft. tall, usually with strongly weeping outer branches clad in bluish green leaves. Trunk nearly black. Flowers variable, usually pink or red. Hardy to 10° (barely) to 15°F.

EUPHORBIA. SPURGE. Huge group of plants including annuals, perennials, shrubs, trees, succulents, a few weeds. Listed here are two semisucculent perennials from the Mediterranean. All have gray green to silvery green leaves symmetrically and densely arranged on stems which bear clusters of greenish yellow to yellow flowers.

Cut off old stems when flowers fade; new ones will already have appeared. All take summer drought, heat, any soil, but need reasonably good drainage.

Euphorbia characias wulfenii

E. characias. Upright stems make a 4-ft. broad bush. Gray green leaves are narrow; flowers clusters are yellow green to lime green in 1½-ft. clusters at stem ends. *E. c. wulfenii* (*E. veneta*) has broader clusters of yellower flowers. Hardy to 10°–15°F.

E. myrsinites. Sprawling branches radiate from central crown. Broad gray blue leaves crowd stems. Flattish clusters of chartreuse to yellow flowers. Excellent foreground border plant; attractive spilling over a wall. Hardy below 0°F., but short-lived in mild winter climates.

EURYOPS pectinatus. Shrubby evergreen perennial to 6 ft. tall with dense clothing of gray green, deeply cut 2-in. leaves and a profusion of yellow 1½- to 2-in. daisies throughout much of the year. Fast growing, tolerant of wind. Easy to maintain; keep old blooms picked off and cut back to side branches to limit growth as needed. Drought tolerant once established. Needs good drainage. Hardy to about 25°F. 'Viridis' is similar, but with green leaves.

Euryops pectinatus

FEIJOA sellowiana. PINEAPPLE GUAVA. Evergreen shrub or small tree to 18–25 ft. with 2- to 3-in. leaves that are bright glossy green above, white beneath. Flowers (May–June) have 4 fleshy white, purple-tinged petals and a showy mass of red stamens in the center. Edible gray green fruit follows in late autumn. (Flowers are edible too.) Sure fruiting varieties are 'Beechwood', 'Coolidge', and 'Nazemetz'. Seedlings commonly offered may not be self-fruitful. Can be shaped as a hedge or pruned into a multitrunked small tree with attractive coppery tan bark. Hardy to 10°–15°F. Probably the hardiest of the so-called tropical fruits. Imported fruit sold as "feijoas."

Feijoa sellowiana

FICUS carica. FIG. Deciduous tree to 15–30 ft.; in cold-winter climates a large shrub with winter protection. Spreading growth with limber branches in youth, picturesque heavy gray trunk in age. Deeply lobed, rough bright green leaves are 4–9 in. long, nearly as wide. Winter branching pattern picturesque; summer shade dense. Excellent ornamental tree. Fruit drop a problem above deck or paving.

Ficus carica

Needs sun, good drainage, any soil; needs little water once established, but occasional irrigation necessary for top fruit production. Most varieties bear a spring and a fall crop and need no pollinating. 'Brown Turkey' and 'Mission' are favorite home garden varieties. Wood hardy to 10°–20°F.; in colder climates, grow in containers and shelter over winter or wrap or bury trunk and main limbs.

FRAXINUS. ASH. Deciduous trees with leaves divided featherwise into many leaflets. Fairly fast growers and good shade, street, or garden trees. Buy named varieties that are seedless to avoid litter.

F. pennsylvanica. GREEN ASH. Moderate grower to 30–40 ft. with compact head. Can take drought, heat, wet or dry soil, extreme cold (−30° to −40°F.). Select seedless varieties such as 'Emerald', 'Marshall', or 'Summit'.

F. velutina. ARIZONA ASH. Southwestern native to 50 ft. Withstands heat, drought. Best known in selected horticultural varieties. Hardy to −10°. 'Modesto', MODESTO ASH, is a vigorous tree to 50 ft. with a 30-ft. spread. Glossy green leaves turn bright yellow in fall. First-class street tree, but overplanting has made it subject to rapid spread of ailments, especially anthracnose following late spring rains, verticillium wilt in agricultural areas. 'Rio Grande', FAN-TEX ASH, has large, dark green, leathery leaflets, tolerates hot winds.

Fraxinus velutina 'Modesto'

FREMONTODENDRON. FREMONTIA, FLANNEL BUSH. Evergreen shrub. Fast growth to 6–20 ft. Leathery leaves are dark green above, fuzzy beneath. Spring flowers profuse, saucer-shaped, yellow or yellow orange. Absolutely drought resistant, intolerant of summer water (although careful watering is necessary until plants are established). Needs good drainage, sun. Best combined with other West Coast native plants. Can take occasional temperature drops to 20°F.

F. californicum. COMMON FLANNEL BUSH. Big show of lemon yellow 1- to 1½-in. flowers in May–June.

F. mexicanum. SOUTHERN FLANNEL BUSH. Larger flowers than *E. californicum* (1½ to 2½ in. across) over a longer period, mass effect not so showy.

Hybrids are 'California Glory', to 20 ft. with 3-in. yellow flowers tinted red outside over a long season; 'Pacific Sunset', deep orange yellow flowers 3½–4 in. wide peaking in late April, May; and 'San Gabriel', much like 'California Glory' but with more deeply cut leaves.

Fremontodendron

GAILLARDIA grandiflora. BLANKET FLOWER. Perennial. Roughish gray green plants 3–4 ft. tall with large single or double daisylike flowers 3–4 in. across in shades of yellow and red with maroon or orange bands. Easy from seed and often self-sow. They need good drainage and sun, will take considerable drought once established. The variety 'Goblin' is 12 in. tall with large, deep red flowers edged yellow. Hardy anywhere, but tends to be short-lived. Taller kinds are excellent cut flowers.

Gaillardia grandiflora

GARRYA elliptica. SILKTASSEL. Evergreen shrub or small tree to 20–30 ft. Leathery leaves are wavy edged, 2½ in. long, deep green above, grayish beneath. Male and female flowers on separate plants; male flowers are showier—clusters of dangling silvery green tassels in midwinter. Female plants (less showy) will produce clusters of inedible grapelike fruit if male plants are nearby. 'James Roof' has exceptionally long male tassels. Good foliage plant, for screening or flower display. Hardy to near 0°F.

Garrya elliptica

GAURA lindheimeri. GAURA. Perennial. Southwestern native 2½–4 ft. tall with branching flower spikes carrying 1-in. white flowers opening from pink buds. Long bloom season with only a few flowers opening at a time. Blossoms drop off cleanly; if flowering spikes are left to seed, plants will look better and self-sown seedlings are less likely to become a nuisance in garden. Tolerates heat, wind, drought. Hardy anywhere. One of few long-lived perennials in Southwest.

Gaura lindheimeri

GAZANIA. Perennial ground cover in warm-winter regions, summer annuals elsewhere. Clumping or trailing, low growing plants produce brilliant display of big daisies in spring and summer. In mild-winter climates bloom may be intermittent throughout the year. Clumping kinds make mounds of evergreen leaves that are dark green above, silvery beneath, often lobed. Flowers are 3 to 4 in. wide in yellow, orange, pink, or white, often with contrasting bands or spots. Many strains are available to grow from seeds; some have flowers up to 5 in. across. Use them as temporary fillers between shrubs, or as small-scale ground covers.

Trailing gazanias (*G. rigens leucolaena*) spread rapidly by long, trailing stems and are useful as ground cover on slopes or level ground. Foliage is gray; flowers are yellow, orange, white, or bronze.

Gazania

Once established, gazanias can get by on two waterings a month (more in desert areas); feed in spring. Divide and replant every 3–4 years, or when plants crowd and die out in patches. Hardy to mid-20's. Not adapted to mild, wet climates.

GEIJERA parviflora. AUSTRALIAN WILLOW. Evergreen tree. Fine-textured tree to 25–30 ft., with upswept branches, drooping branchlets and very narrow, drooping leaves to 6 in. long. Leaves give effect of weeping willow, cast light shade. Deep rooting on well-drained soil and quite drought tolerant once established; grows faster with ample water. Pest free and requires little pruning. Useful street, patio, or garden tree. Hardy to 20°–25°F.

Geijera parviflora

GENISTA. BROOM. Deciduous shrubs, but with green branches for evergreen look, profusion of bright yellow, sweet pea-shaped flowers in spring and early summer. Kinds listed here are attractive ground or bank covers, wall spillers, and large rock garden shrubs. They need full sun (light shade in hottest summer climates), good drainage and endure poor rocky soil, heat, ocean winds, and drought. Hardy to 0°F. or lower.

G. lydia. Grows 2 ft. tall, with spreading, sprawling habit.

G. pilosa. To 1–1½ ft. tall, with 7-ft. spread. 'Vancouver Gold' is a choice selection.

Genista lydia

GINKGO biloba. GINKGO, MAIDENHAIR TREE. Deciduous tree usually 35–50 ft. tall, occasionally to 80 ft. with leathery, fan-shaped leaves 1–4 in. wide. Leaves turn brilliant yellow in fall, drop quickly and cleanly. Growth open and irregular in youth, filling out in maturity. Pest free and tolerant of city smoke and dust. Trees need water until 10–20 ft. tall, then become self-sufficient if planted in deep, well drained soil. Plant only grafted male trees; females produce messy, smelly fruit (which does have, however, an edible nutlike kernel). Hardy anywhere, but not adapted to hot, windy desert sites.

Ginkgo biloba

GLEDITSIA triacanthos. HONEY LO-CUST. Deciduous trees of rapid growth to 35–70 ft. with erect trunk and spreading, arching branches. Leaves divided into many oval, inch-long leaflets which turn yellow and drop early in fall. Late to leaf out in spring. Trunks and branches armed with vicious thorns on wild trees, but selected garden varieties are thornless and also lack the foot-long, beanlike seed pods. Good lawn trees because of light shade, long deciduous period. Because of form, sometimes used as substitute for elms where elm disease is a problem. Not good trees for narrow curb strips; roots can heave paving. Hardy anywhere, but likes climates with clearly marked winter, hot summer. Takes heat, cold, moderate drought.

Gleditsia triacanthos

'Halka', 'Imperial', 'Moraine', 'Shademaster', 'Skyline', and 'Trueshade' are selected forms used for shade. 'Rubylace' has deep red, 'Sunburst' brilliant yellow new growth.

GREVILLEA. Evergreen shrubs or trees from Australia. Large, highly variable group, with new species and hybrids arriving frequently from Australia. Not all are adaptable to dense, alkaline soils, but many are attractive enough to warrant experiment. Both listed here have fine-textured foliage and narrow, tubular flowers in tight clusters. All endure poor, rocky soil if drainage is good, sun, heat, and drought once established. Subject to iron-deficiency chlorosis in dense, alkaline soils or soggy soil conditions. Most are hardy to about 25°F.

Grevillea 'Noellii'

G. 'Noellii'. Shrub to 4 ft. tall, 4–5 ft. wide, with angled, nearly horizontal branching, medium green, inch-long needlelike leaves, clusters of pink and white flowers in spring. Useful as low, informal hedge. Some drought tolerance, but can endure more water than most.

G. robusta. SILK OAK. Fast growing tree to 50–60 ft. or more with fernlike leaves and (when mature) striking clusters of golden orange flowers in spring. Symmetrical when young, spreading and picturesque in age, usually with a few heavy, wide-spreading limbs. Subject to wind breakage; prune hard to fatten and shorten branches. Good desert tree. Mature trees can survive 16°F.

GYMNOCLADUS dioica. KENTUCKY COFFEE TREE. Deciduous tree to 50 ft. with relatively few, stout branches when mature. Fast growth as a sapling, eventually slowing. Leaves are 1½–3 ft. long, divided into many 1- to 3-in. leaflets, deep green in summer, yellow in fall. Inconspicuous flowers are followed by 6- to 10-in. reddish brown seed pods containing hard black seeds. which were once roasted and ground as a coffee substitute. Tropical-looking foliage, picturesque winter silhouette make for an attractive tree in cold-winter climates. Hardy well below 0°F.

Gymnocladus dioica

HAKEA. Evergreen shrubs or small trees from Australia, tough, tolerant, heat and wind resistant plants that thrive in poor (but well drained) soils. Hardy to about 20°F.

H. laurina. SEA URCHIN, PINCUSHION TREE. Small, dense, rounded big shrub or small tree to 30 ft. Narrow, gray green 6-in. leaves, sometimes red-edged. Winter flowers resemble round crimson pincushions stuck with golden pins. Stake when young to prevent toppling in wind.

Hakea laurina

H. suaveolens. SWEET HAKEA. Dense, broad, erect shrub to 10–20 ft. Dark green 4-in. leaves are divided into stiff, sharp-pointed segments; effect is that of a pine. Small, fragrant white flowers in fall, winter. Fast growing barrier or screen; can be shaped into small tree.

H. victoria. ROYAL HAKEA. Narrow shrub to 9 ft. tall with broad, flat, cupped leaves. Leaves are leathery, toothed, marked with yellow and orange.

HELENIUM autumnale. SNEEZE-WEED. Perennial 1–6 ft. tall depending on variety. Many erect leafy stems crowned with daisylike flowers summer through fall. Colors include yellow, orange, red, copper, all with a dark brown center. Needs sun, blooms best where summers are hot. Endures drought, some neglect. Hardy anywhere.

Helenium autumnale

HELIANTHEMUM nummularium. SUNROSE. Evergreen shrublets to 6–8 in. tall, spreading to 3 ft. Leaves ½–1 in. long, bright green or gray green depending on variety. Many named varieties with single or double flowers in white, pink, rose, red, orange, yellow; each bloom lasts only a day, but new buds open over a long period—spring to early summer in mild-winter climates, late spring to midsummer elsewhere.

Helianthemum nummularium

Plant sunroses on banks, in rock gardens, atop walls. They need average soil, good drainage, light watering and tolerate heat and some drought once established. In cold-winter areas, protect foliage with a light covering of evergreen boughs. Hardy below 0°F.

HELIANTHUS salicifolius (H. orgyalis). This perennial sunflower, native to Missouri, Oklahoma, Texas, and Colorado, has an odd, shaggy, tropical look. Its stems (3–6, even 10 ft. tall) are closely packed with very narrow, drooping leaves 6 in. to 1 ft. long. Stems within clump are branched only at top, opening into a broad shower of brown-centered, bright yellow 2-in. daisies. Effect is that of a tall green fountain erupting into a rain of flowers. This odd but spectacular plant tolerates heat and some drought when established.

Helianthus salicifolius

HELICHRYSUM petiolatum. Shrubby perennial. Woody-based plants to 2 ft. with trailing stems that extend 4 ft. or more to either side. Leaves 1 in. long, covered with white wool, are the feature; flowers insignificant and may be removed. Use as a ground cover or as contrast with green foliage; white branches weave attractively through darker leaves. Needs good drainage, average soil, sun, some trimming to control growth. Endures heat, drought. Hardy to 28°F.

Helichrysum petiolatum

HELLEBORUS. HELLEBORE. Evergreen perennials. Long-lived plants for shade or part shade. Attractive divided foliage and oddly pretty flowers. They need reasonably good soil and good drainage. The following species tolerate long dry spells, but not absolute summer-long drought.

H. foetidus. Grows to 1½ ft., with leaves divided fanwise into 7–11 narrow, very dark green segments. Dome-shaped clusters of inch-wide, light green flowers with purple margins appear February–April. Cut off withered stalks to groom. Will self-sow where adapted. Hardy below 0°F.

Helleborus lividus corsicus

H. lividus corsicus. CORSICAN HELLEBORE. Grows to 3 ft., with leaves divided into 3 pale blue green, sharply toothed segments. Clusters of large, light chartreuse flowers appear in winter and spring in mildest winters, early spring in Northwest. Flowers remain attractive for a long time. Stands more sun than *H. foetidus.* Hardy to 10°–15°F.

HETEROMELES arbutifolia. TOYON. Evergreen shrub or small tree. Grows 6–10 ft. tall as a shrub; can be trained as a 15- to 25-ft. tree. Leathery, glossy dark green leaves are 2–4 in. long, sharply toothed. Flattish clusters of small white flowers in summer are followed by a fine show of bright red berries in late fall, winter. Endures much drought, but tolerates summer water, needs it in desert climates. Berries attract birds. Full sun or partial shade, good drainage. Tolerates occasional temperature drops to near 0°F.

Heteromeles arbutifolia

HIBISCUS syriacus. ROSE OF SHARON, SHRUB ALTHAEA. Deciduous shrub to 10–12 ft., easily trained as single-trunk small tree. Leaves are sharply toothed, sometimes 3-lobed; flowers, single or double, appear in summer and early fall. Colors include white, pink, red, purple, near-blue. Single flowers are showier than doubles, opening wider, but they produce a big crop of seed pods, often self-sow where year-round water is supplied. ('Diana', a large white single, produces no seed.)

Hibiscus syriacus

Will grow in sun or light shade; moderate water best, but will take much drought if established. For less-crowded growth and bigger flowers, prune previous year's growth back to 2 buds in winter.

HIPPOPHAE rhamnoides. SEA BUCK-THORN. Deciduous shrub. Grows to 10–15 ft. with willowlike leaves to 3 in. long, gray green above, silvery beneath. Flowers inconspicuous, but female plants bear profusion of bright yellow orange fruits if pollinated by a nearby male plant. Fruit lasts all winter (birds will not eat it). Withstands heat, wind, seaside conditions, cold, drought. Likes sun, good drainage. Hardy well below 0°F.

Hippophae rhamnoides

HYPERICUM calycinum. AARON'S BEARD, CREEPING ST. JOHNSWORT. Evergreen shrub, partially deciduous in coldest climates. Tough underground stems send up 12-in. stems with short-stalked oval leaves to 4 in. long. Foliage medium green in sun, yellow green in shade. Bright yellow flowers 3 in. across. Useful as ground cover in difficult situations; grows in sun or shade, takes much water or considerable drought, can compete with tree roots. Spreads rapidly and is good erosion control on banks. Can invade other plantings unless curbed. Mow every 2–3 years to encourage fresh growth. Hardy to 0°–10°F.

Hypericum calycinum

IRIS. Large and diverse group of plants, some with bulbs, some with creeping rhizomes. All mentioned below have fans of flat, sword-shaped leaves and showy flowers of complex structure. Many species are grown by dedicated amateurs, but drought-tolerant kinds generally available are hybrids in one of three general classes.

Bearded irises. These are the most commonly grown, and hundreds of varieties are available in nearly every color of the rainbow. All have thick, branching rhizomes that eventually produce clumps of gray green, sword-shaped leaves in fan arrangement. Flowers have three erect segments (standards), and three drooping or horizontal segments (falls); the latter have tufts of hair (the beard). Most widely grown kinds are tall bearded (2½–4 ft. tall).

Tall Bearded Iris

They need full sun (light shade in hottest areas), good drainage; most well-drained soils are adequate. Established clumps need little water during the summer—2 or 3 soakings in hot areas will suffice. Hardy anywhere (mulch in very coldest climates).

Pacific Coast irises. These are hybrids between several species native to California, Oregon, and Washington. They form clumps of bright green leaves 1½–2 ft. tall; flower stems are 1–2 ft. tall, often branched, and carry 2 to several flowers in white, cream, yellow, lavender, blue, and purple. They like full sun in mild-summer western gardens, but will take considerable shade. Where summers are hot, part shade is best. Established plants need no summer water, but will accept occasional irrigation if drainage is perfect. Most can take occasional drops in temperature to near 0°F.

Spuria iris. This complex group of hybrids makes clumps of erect, narrow sword-shaped leaves. Flowers of white, yellow, lavender, blue, bronze, or buff open on stalks from 1–6 ft. tall, depending on variety. Flowers resemble florists' Dutch iris in form. Plants need rich soil, ample water until bloom is over, little or no water thereafter. Hardy anywhere.

JACARANDA mimosifolia. JACARANDA. Deciduous or semievergreen tree, 25–40 ft. tall, with open, irregular, often multitrunked habit. Finely cut, fernlike leaves usually drop in early spring; new foliage may appear immediately or wait until bloom—usually in June, occasionally later. Lavender blue 2-in. trumpet flowers in 8-in.-long clusters make a fine show. Accepts most soils; does not bloom well in path of cool ocean winds. Not completely drought tolerant, but thrives best on infrequent, deep irrigation. Young plants tender below 25°F.; established trees with hard wood somewhat hardier.

Jacaranda mimosifolia

JUGLANS. WALNUT. Deciduous trees with leaves divided featherwise into many leaflets. Nuts have bony shells and are encased in leathery husks. Three western American species are highly drought tolerant and, although not usually sold commercially, are worth keeping if they occur as natives.

J. californica, native to southern California, is shrubby or a small tree 15–30 ft. tall. ***J. hindsii***, CALIFORNIA BLACK WALNUT, is a broad-crowned tree 30-60 ft. tall from northern California. ***J. major*** (*J. rupestris major*), NOGAL or ARIZONA WALNUT, is a 50-ft. tree from Arizona, New Mexico, and northern Mexico.

Juglans hindsii

JUNIPERUS. JUNIPER. Evergreen shrubs or trees with needlelike or scalelike foliage and fleshy, berrylike cones. There is a juniper for almost any landscape use; forms are varied, from prostrate ground covers to sprawling, conical, or rigidly columnar shrubs, even trees. Color varies from deep green to gray green, blue green, and golden. Some varieties have creamy variegation. Select and place varieties with care; many grow larger than expected, and can crowd paths and other plantings or obscure windows and doorways.

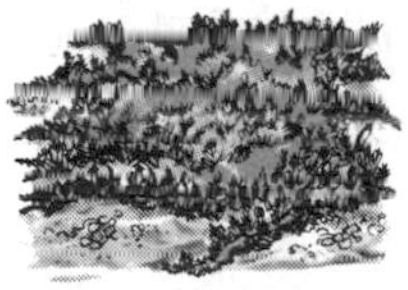

Juniperus horizontalis

All are plants that get along with minimal care. They thrive in any reasonably well drained soil and all but a few are hardy anywhere (those few are not sold in areas where they are tender).

Best in full sun, but will take some shade in hottest areas. Established plants need little or no supplementary water; most profit from an occasional deep irrigation. They are subject to root rot (yellowing and collapse) if soil remains soggy. Avoid planting where their roots are reached by lawn sprinklers.

Varieties are too numerous to mention; well-stocked nurseries offer a wide choice of plants that will thrive in your region. Most grow anywhere; the few that do not are not likely to be sold in very hot or cold regions.

KNIPHOFIA uvaria *(Tritoma uvaria)*. RED-HOT POKER. Perennial. Big clumps of coarse, grasslike leaves produce 3- to 6-ft. stalks topped by a dense cluster of drooping tubular orange red or yellow flowers. Bloom season spring through summer. Smaller, more refined garden varieties have flowers of coral, creamy white. Use among shrubs or in big perennial borders. Cut back old leaves in fall and remove spent flower stalks. If flower production drops off, divide plants in spring. Likes sun, heat; tolerates considerable drought. Hardy anywhere, but not planted in desert regions.

Kniphofia uvaria

KOELREUTERIA paniculata. GOLDENRAIN TREE. Deciduous tree. Slow to moderate growth rate to 20–35 ft., with open branching, giving light shade. Leaves to 15 in. long, divided into 1- to 3-in. lobed or toothed leaflets. Loose clusters 8–14 in. long of small yellow flowers in summer. Ornamental fruit consists of fat, papery capsules like little Japanese lanterns; these turn from buff to brown and hang on tree a long time.

Good small to medium tree for difficult soils; will take heat, cold, wind, and drought when established. Hardy well below 0°F.

Koelreuteria paniculata

LAGERSTROEMIA indica. CRAPE MYRTLE. Deciduous shrub or tree to 30 ft. tall. Attractive trunk, with smooth pale brown or gray bark peeling to reveal pinkish new bark. Leaves unfurl bronzy light green, turn deep glossy green, then yellow, orange, or red before dropping.

Crinkled 1½-in. flowers in 6- to 12-in. clusters appear from July to September. Colors are red, pink, lavender, purple, and white. Crape myrtle likes full sun and heat, blooms poorly and gets mildew in cool-summer areas. Varieties named after Indian tribes are resistant to mildew; look for 'Catawba', 'Cherokee', 'Muskogee', 'Natchez', and the like.

Lagerstroemia indica

Habit is variable; some forms are dwarf (5–7 ft. tall), and some are prostrate or trailing. The last named can be used as ground cover or even as hanging basket plants.

Water infrequently but deeply once plants are established, and treat chlorosis or leaf burn by occasional leaching and applications of iron. Feed lightly and prune in dormant season to increase next summer's flowering wood. Tops are hardy to occasional drops to 0°F.; roots are hardy, and plants are occasionally grown as perennials in cold-winter areas.

LANTANA. Evergreen sprawling, mounding, or vining shrubs (deciduous in hard frosts). Tight, round clusters of flowers appear over a long season—all year in mildest climates. Needs sun, ordinary soil, little feeding, hard pruning in spring to control tangle and woodiness. Use as bank or ground cover, low hedges or dividers, beds of flower color. Damaged in upper 20's but possibly with good recovery. Use as annuals elsewhere.

L. camara. Ancestor of most garden lantanas. Shrubby, to 6 ft., with flowers of yellow, orange, or red—frequently in the same cluster.

L. montevidensis (L. sellowiana). Sprawling or trailing plant with prostrate branches to 6 ft. long. Dark green leaves often tinted purplish; lilac flowers come in 1½-in. clusters. Ground cover, wall cover hanging basket plant. Somewhat hardier than other lantanas.

Lantana montevidensis

L. hybrids. Some are forms of *L. camara,* others are hybrids between it and *L. montevidensis.* Height ranges from 1½–6 ft., width to 6–8 ft. Colors run from cream and yellow through pink and orange to red. Taller kinds can be staked as small decorative trees; low, spreading varieties are among the most colorful ground or bank covers.

LAURUS nobilis. SWEET BAY, GRECIAN LAUREL. Evergreen shrub or tree to 12–40 ft. Naturally a dense, tapering cone, but can be trained into a single- or multi-stemmed tree or pruned into hedge, screen, or topiary shape. Leaves, 2–4 in. long and leathery, are the bay leaves used in cooking. Small yellow flowers are followed by clusters of black berries. Ordinary soil with good drainage, full sun (except in hottest desert areas); needs little water once established. Hardy to 15°–20°F.

Laurus nobilis

LAVANDULA. LAVENDER. Shrubs or shrubby perennials with gray or gray green foliage and lavender or purple fragrant flowers used in perfumery and sachets. Depending on size of plant, use as hedge, low screen, edging, or in borders with other drought-tolerant plants such as rockrose, sunrose, rosemary, and verbena. All need sun, good drainage, little water or fertilizer. Prune after bloom to keep plants compact.

Lavandula angustifolia

L. angustifolia. ENGLISH LAVENDER. Narrow 2-in., smooth edged leaves are gray. Flowers are densely clustered at the top of 1½- to 2-ft. stems in late spring, summer. Dwarf varieties for edging are 'Hidcote', 1 ft. tall with silvery gray leaves and deep purple flowers; 'Munstead', 1½ ft. tall with deep lavender blue flowers; and 'Twickel Purple', 2–3 ft., with purple flowers in fanlike spikes. Hardy to near 0°F.

L. dentata. FRENCH LAVENDER. Gray green leaves with square-toothed edges, lavender purple flowers in short clusters crowned with a tuft of purple petallike bracts. Almost everblooming in mild-winter regions. *L. d. candicans* has larger leaves covered with grayish white down on young foliage. Hardy to 20°–25°F.

L. stoechas. SPANISH LAVENDER. Gray-leafed plant 1½–3 ft. tall with narrow leaves and dense clusters of dark purple flowers topped by a tuft of large purple bracts. Hardy to near 0°F.

LEPTOSPERMUM laevigatum. AUSTRALIAN TEA TREE. Evergreen shrub or small tree to 30 ft. tall and as wide. When allowed to grow naturally, makes a picturesque tree with twisting, leaning or nearly prostrate trunk and branches that carry spreading or weeping boughs with dull green or gray green leaves 1 in. long, less than half as wide. Small white flowers appear in spring. Pinched and pruned when young, makes a dense clipped hedge or screen plant. Needs well drained, slightly acid soil; accepts full sun and strongest ocean winds, little water. Hardy to 20°–25°F.

Leptospermum laevigatum

LEUCOPHYLLUM frutescens. TEXAS RANGER, TEXAS SAGE, CENIZO. Evergreen shrub 6–8 ft. or taller, with gray white foliage and rose purple, bell-shaped, 1-in. flowers in summer. Excellent desert plant, enduring heat, wind, alkaline soil (if well drained); needs summer heat for good bloom.

Use as individual plant or as clipped screen or hedge. 'Compactum' is smaller and denser. 'Green Cloud' has gray green leaves, 'White Cloud' silvery foliage and white flowers. Hardy to 10°F.

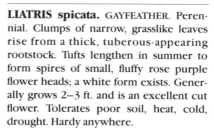

Leucophyllum frutescens

LIATRIS spicata. GAYFEATHER. Perennial. Clumps of narrow, grasslike leaves rise from a thick, tuberous-appearing rootstock. Tufts lengthen in summer to form spires of small, fluffy rose purple flower heads; a white form exists. Generally grows 2–3 ft. and is an excellent cut flower. Tolerates poor soil, heat, cold, drought. Hardy anywhere.

Liatris spicata

LIMONIUM (Statice). SEA LAVENDER. Perennials. Clumps of large, leathery leaves give rise to airy sheaves of tiny, papery-textured flowers that are excellent for cutting and drying. They thrive in ordinary well drained soil in sun, often volunteering from seed where adapted.

L. latifolium. To 2½ ft. tall, with clouds of tiny white and bluish flowers up to a yard wide floating above a clump of 10-in.-long leaves. Hardy anywhere; not adapted in low and intermediate desert climates.

Limonium perezii

L. perezii. Leaves up to 1 ft. long; long summer bloom, with flowers of rich purple and white. Clusters can reach 3 ft. tall and as wide. Damaged at 25°F., but seedlings grow fast.

LINUM. FLAX. Perennials to 2 ft. with upright, freely branching stems, narrow wispy leaves, and a profusion of cup-shaped blue flowers. Each bloom lasts a day, but replacements keep coming on. Needs light, well drained soil in sun. Not long lived, but easy to grow from seed. Needs little water or feeding. Use in borders or as bulb cover.

Linum perenne

L. narbonense. Flowers are large (to 1¾ in.), azure blue with white eye.

L. perenne. PERENNIAL BLUE FLAX. To 2 ft., usually leafless below. Branching clusters of light blue flowers May–September. Flowers close in shade or late in the day.

LOBELIA laxiflora. Perennial with 2 ft. stems arising from creeping underground rootstocks. Leaves are narrow, dark green. Open clusters of orange red flowers appear over a long summer season. Once established, tolerates much neglect; often persists in abandoned gardens. Hardy to occasional drops into 10°–15°F. range.

Lobelia laxiflora

LOBULARIA maritima (Alyssum maritimum). SWEET ALYSSUM. Annual, but self-sowing and tough enough to become a permanent performer in dry gardens; often used in roadside wild flower or erosion control mixes. Low, freely branching, to 1 ft. tall, with clustered white, honey scented flowers. Easy, quick growing (blooms in 6 weeks from seed), takes almost any soil, very little water once well rooted. Prefers full sun, endures light shade. Shearing plants back a month after peak bloom may result in a second bloom.

Lobularia maritima

Garden varieties are dwarfer (some only 2–4 in. tall), and some are lavender, lavender pink, or deep purple. Self-sown plants tend to revert to white. Use as temporary ground cover, bank cover, filler between stepping stones, along roadsides, over bulbs.

LONICERA. HONEYSUCKLE. Evergreen or deciduous vines or shrubs, some tolerant of drought. All have tubular flowers, but not all are fragrant.

L. japonica 'Halliana'. HALL'S HONEYSUCKLE, JAPANESE HONEYSUCKLE. Evergreen vine, deciduous in coldest regions. Rampant growth to 15 ft. or more in height; sprawling on the ground, stems will root and cover large areas quickly. Can be a pest where year-round rains occur. Deep

Lonicera japonica 'Halliana'

green, oval leaves; tubular, lipped white flowers aging pale yellow have a rich, sweet fragrance. Use as ground cover, screening on chain link fence or trellis, for casual charm on informal rail fence. Tolerates most soils, drought when established. Cut back hard periodically to prevent buildup of dead stems. Hardy except in the very coldest climates.

L. tatarica. TATARIAN HONEYSUCKLE. Deciduous shrub useful in coldest climates (can withstand -30° to -40°F.). To 10 ft., with dark green or bluish green leaves, small pink to rose flowers in late spring or summer, and bright red fruit. Useful for screen, background, windbreak.

L. xylosteoides. Deciduous shrubby honeysuckle hybrid known chiefly through 'Clavey's Dwarf' variety, a 3-ft. (rarely to 6 ft.) shrub with blue green leaves and inconspicuous white flowers. Drought tolerant, and as hardy as *L. tatarica*.

LYONOTHAMNUS floribundus asplenifolius. FERNLEAF CATALINA IRONWOOD. Evergreen tree to 30–60 ft. tall. Slender erect trunk has red brown bark that peels off in long strips. Leaves 4–6 in. long are divided into deeply notched leaflets, deep green above, gray green beneath. Small white flowers in flat 8- to 18-in. clusters are showy, but should be cut off before they turn brown.

Tree needs good drainage and can stand summer-long drought in cool-summer climates. Hardy to about 20°F. Erect habit and shreddy red bark give effect of redwood.

Lyonothamnus floribundus asplenifolius

MACFADYENA unguis-cati (Doxantha unguis-cati, Bignonia tweediana). CAT'S CLAW, YELLOW TRUMPET VINE. Partly deciduous vine, completely so where winters are cold. Climbs to 25–40 ft., clings to any support (stone, wood, stucco, concrete) by clawlike tendrils at ends of leaves. Glossy green leaves divided into two 2-in. leaflets. Yellow trumpet flowers 2 in. long, 1½ in. wide appear in spring.

Macfadyena unguis-cati

Loves heat and tolerates drought once established. Prune some stems nearly to ground from time to time to encourage even cover. Without such care growth will concentrate at tops of stems. Hardy to about 15°F.

MACLURA pomifera. OSAGE ORANGE. Deciduous tree of fast growth to 60 ft. Habit open, spreading, with thorny branches, 5-in. medium green leaves. If male plants are present, females produce inedible 4-in. fruits that look like bumpy yellow-green oranges (flower arrangers like them). Stands shearing and is usually grown as big hedge, living fence, or screen. Easily propagated by seed, cuttings, or root cuttings. Can be trained into shade tree. Tolerates heat, wind, cold, poor soil, some alkalinity, drought. Needs some water to get started. Hardy anywhere.

Maclura pomifera

MAHONIA. Evergreen shrubs sometimes classified as barberries (*Berberis*), but differing in always having 3 or more leaflets to a leaf. Stems have no spines, but leaves have sharp-toothed edges. Yellow flowers in rounded to spikelike clusters. Some of the hardiest broadleaf evergreen shrubs are found here. All listed here tolerate shade or sun and are drought tolerant. Planting of some species is prohibited in wheat-growing states; consult local authorities.

M. aquifolium. OREGON GRAPE. Evergreen shrub to 6 ft. or more, spreading slowly by underground stems. Leaves 4–

Mahonia aquifolium

10 in. long with glossy, deep green spiny-toothed leaflets 1–2½ in. long. New foliage is bronzy red, and in winter all foliage takes on bronzy or purplish tones, especially in the sun. An occasional leaf turns orange or red before falling. Clusters of flowers 2–3 in. long in early spring give way to blue black fruit with gray bloom. Sour but edible fruit makes good jelly. Good foundation shrub, woodland plant (but can take sun except in hottest climates), low border or barrier. Hardy well below 0°F. 'Compacta', to 2 ft., spreads freely to make low masses.

M. pinnata. CALIFORNIA HOLLY GRAPE. Similar to Oregon grape but with spinier, more crinkly leaves, usually taller growth. More drought tolerant than Oregon grape.

M. repens. CREEPING MAHONIA. Creeps by underground stems, sending up erect stems to 3 ft., usually much less. Leaves dull bluish green. Rocky Mountain native; hardy many degrees below 0°F.

MELALEUCA. Evergreen shrubs or trees with narrow, often needlelike leaves and tight flower clusters that consist mostly of stamens; effect is that of a small bottlebrush. Ones listed below all tolerate much or little water and stand up to heat, wind, poor soil, and salt air. All are hardy to around 25°F.

M. linariifolia. FLAXLEAF PAPERBARK. Tree to 30 ft. with broad, spreading crown with white, peeling bark and thin branchlets covered with thin, needlelike green or blue green leaves. Fluffy spikes of white flowers are numerous enough to look like snow on the branches in late spring or early summer.

Melaleuca linariifolia

M. nesophila. PINK MELALEUCA. Big shrub or tree to 30 ft. with gnarled, picturesque trunk and branches covered with thick, spongy bark. Leaves are gray green, roundish, 1 in. long. Inch-long mauve flower clusters fade to white and yellow; blossoms form nearly year-round. Use as tree, screen, or clipped hedge.

M. quinquenervia. CAJEPUT TREE. Erect, open growth to 20–40 ft., with weeping branchlets and thick, spongy bark that can be peeled off in sheets. Leaves narrow, 2–4 in. long, pale green, turning purplish in cold weather. Flowers white (rarely pink or purple). Useful as street tree or in groves. Caution: In Florida, where it is called PUNK TREE, and possibly in other warm regions where rain occurs the year around, this tree can become a pest, seeding itself and driving out native shrubs and trees.

MELAMPODIUM leucanthum. BLACKFOOT DAISY. Perennial. Southwestern native grows 1 ft. tall, equally wide, with narrow gray leaves and clouds of inch-wide white, yellow-centered daisies. In mild-winter areas, intermittent bloom in winter, heavy bloom April–October with some water; spring and summer bloom only in colder regions. Needs good drainage, occasional cutting back. Short lived. Hardy to 0°F. Plants in bloom are showy and among the most useful perennials in the desert. They are scarcely known outside that region.

Melampodium leucanthum

MELIA azedarach. CHINABERRY. Deciduous tree of spreading habit to 30–50 ft. Leaves 1–3 ft. long, divided into many 1- to 2-in. toothed leaflets. Loose clusters of fragrant lilac flowers in spring, early summer, followed by yellow, hard, berrylike fruit ½ in. across. Reputed poisonous, but birds eat it. Attractive bare branches strung with berries are picturesque winter sight. 'Umbraculiformis', TEXAS UMBRELLA TREE, is more common in the West and Southwest. It grows to a dense dome to 30 ft. which seldom blooms or fruits. Among the toughest of trees for heat, wind, drought, poor soil. Hardy to about 10°F.

Melia azedarach 'Umbraculiformis'

METROSIDEROS excelsus. NEW ZEALAND CHRISTMAS TREE. Evergreen tree to 30 ft. or more, shrubby when young; needs careful training to make into a single-stem tree. Leaves glossy green on young plants, dark green above and white-woolly beneath on older plants. Dark red flowers cluster at ends of branches in midsummer. Needs regular irrigation first 2 years, afterwards self-sufficient in the mild coastal conditions it needs to survive. Hardy to only the lightest frosts.

Metrosideros excelsus

MIRABILIS jalapa. FOUR O'CLOCK. Perennial (annual in cold-winter climates). Erect, many-branched stems arise from tuberous roots to make a shrublike 3- to 4-ft. plant. Flowers are red, yellow, or white, sometimes mixed on the same plant or even on the same flower. Sow seeds in sun in early spring for bloom summer-fall. Self-sows, but seedlings tend to revert to plain red. A survivor plant, often seen on vacant lots or in abandoned gardens. Tubers hardy to nearly 0°F.

Mirabilis jalapa

MYOPORUM parvifolium. Evergreen prostrate shrub 3 in. tall, spreading to 9 ft.; branches root where they touch soil. Narrow leaves ½–1 in. long, densely clothing stems. Small summer white flowers followed by purple berries. Fast ground cover for well drained soils. Likes heat, withstands drought but looks better with some summer water. Hardy to about 15°F. Named varieties are 'Davis' and 'Putah Creek'.

Myoporum parvifolium

MYRSINE africana. AFRICAN BOXWOOD. Evergreen shrub 3–8 ft. tall, easily maintained as dense, formal 3–4 ft. shrub with minimal pinching or pruning. Vertical dark red stems closely set with dark green, glossy, roundish ½-in. leaves. Takes sun or light shade. Use as low hedge or formal clipped plant. Endures moderate drought. Hardy to 15°–20°F.

Myrsine africana

NANDINA domestica. HEAVENLY BAMBOO, SACRED BAMBOO. Evergreen shrub to 6–8 ft., with erect stems from underground rootstocks, intricately divided foliage, open growth habit. New foliage reddish on expanding, then light green, turning bronzy or red in winter, especially in sun and with some frost. Clusters of small white or pinkish flowers open on branch ends in late spring or early summer. Red berries may follow if plants are grouped.

Nandina domestica

Especially useful where a narrow, erect plant is called for; good screen, informal hedge. Many named varieties are available. Dwarf forms sold as 'Nana', 'Nana Compacta', 'Nana Purpurea', 'Pygmaea'. 'Harbour Dwarf' grows 1½–2 ft. tall, spreads rapidly to make a good ground cover. Thrives in shade and sun (except in hottest climates), likes water but tolerates drought when established, even dry shade in competition with tree roots. Loses leaves at 10°F.; killed to ground at 5°, but comes back.

NERIUM oleander. OLEANDER. Evergreen shrub to 8–20 ft. tall and equally broad, trainable as a single- or multistemmed small tree. A basic plant for hot, dry climates, withstanding reflected heat, wind, poor drainage, and soil with high salt content. Leaves 4–12 in. long, narrow, shiny, leathery. Flowers at twig and branch ends are 2–3 in. wide, clustered, white to pink, red, salmon, pale yellow. Single-flowered kinds drop blossoms cleanly; double flowers tend to hang on and dry up. Dwarf forms 3–4 ft. tall are less hardy, except for variety 'Little Red'. All are poisonous in every part.

Nerium oleander

Use as screen, windbreak, border, background, tub plant, small tree. Hardy to 15°–20°F.

OCHNA serrulata (*O. multiflora*). BIRD'S EYE BUSH, MICKEY MOUSE PLANT. Evergreen shrub. Slow growth to 4–8 ft. Leaves 2–5 in. long, leathery, fine-toothed, bronze on opening, deep green when mature. Yellow flowers shaped like buttercups turn to attractive red fleshy fruiting bodies carrying shiny black seeds like miniature ears. Likes part shade, acid soil. Stands drought when established. Good small espalier. Hardy to 20°–25°F.

Ochna serrulata

OENOTHERA berlandieri (*O. speciosa childsii*). MEXICAN EVENING PRIMROSE. Perennial. Long spring and summer show of 1½-in. rose pink flowers on 10- to 12-in. stems, which die back after bloom. Spreads freely by underground rootstocks, can invade other plantings if not curbed. A real survivor; needs little or no care once established. Hardy anywhere.

Oenothera berlandieri

OLEA europaea. OLIVE. Evergreen tree. Slow growth to 25–30 ft. tall (although young trees put on height quickly), with single or multiple trunks. Old trees develop picturesque gnarled trunks. Narrow, willowlike leaves are silvery gray green. Fruits ripen and drop in late fall and winter; they stain paving if not removed. Lessen problem by thinning branches, spraying with a fruit control hormone, or shaking off fruit onto a tarpaulin. Fruit edible only with careful processing. For olive trees without fruit, look for scarce and expensive variety 'Swan Hill'.

Olea europaea

Grow in full sun. Trees thrive in deep, rich soil but accept poor, thin, rocky soil of low fertility. They like heat but perform acceptably near the ocean. Hardy to 15°F.

OSMANTHUS. Evergreen shrubs with leathery leaves and tiny, very fragrant flowers. Need water to get started, then moderately drought tolerant. Plant in sun or light to medium shade; will tolerate most soils, including clays, if reasonably well drained. Slow to moderate growers, long lived. Can be sheared or shaped.

O. fragrans. SWEET OLIVE. Compact growth to 10 ft. or more. Leaves glossy, medium green, to 4 in. long. Tiny white flowers appear sporadically throughout year in mild areas, powerfully scented of apricot. *O. f. aurantiacus* is similar, but has orange flowers in early to mid-autumn. Hardy to 15°F.

Osmanthus fragrans

O. heterophyllus (*O. aquifolium, O. ilicifolium*). HOLLY-LEAF OSMANTHUS. Dense upright growth to 6–8 ft. or much more, with dark green leaves strongly toothed like holly. 'Variegatus' has leaves edged white. Both make good hedges, barriers, screens. Hardy to 0°F.

OSTEOSPERMUM fruticosum. TRAILING AFRICAN DAISY, FREEWAY DAISY. Evergreen perennial or subshrub. Grows rapidly, covering 2- to 4-ft. circle in one year from a rooted cutting; trailing branches root as they grow. Grows 6–12 in. tall, with medium green foliage; lilac daisy flowers (which fade to nearly white on second day) have dark purple centers. White and dark purple varieties are available. Bloom intermittent throughout year, heaviest in late winter, spring, and fall. Needs sun, good drainage. Endures drought once established; grows faster and is fire retardant if well watered. Use as bank or ground cover, spilling over a wall. Hardy to 15°F.

Osteospermum fruticosum

PAPAVER orientale. ORIENTAL POPPY. Perennial. Coarse-leafed, hairy plant with stems 2–4 ft. tall carrying big (to 6-inch) flowers of scarlet, orange, salmon, pink, or white flowers (some bicolored) in mid- to late spring. Plants avoid drought by going dormant in summer. New growth appears in fall, lives over winter, and develops rapidly in spring. Hardy in cold-winter climates, but short lived where winters are warm.

Papaver orientale

PARKINSONIA aculeata. JERUSALEM THORN, MEXICAN PALO VERDE. Deciduous tree to 15–30 ft., with picturesque branching habit, yellow green bark, sparse foliage that filters sun rather than blocking it. Leaves 6–9 in. long, with many tiny leaflets that fall in drought or cold. Yellow flowers in loose 3- to 7-in. clusters in spring, then intermittently through the year. Tolerates drought, alkaline soil, needs staking and training to assume tree form. Useful desert tree, but litter drop a problem above hard surfaces. Hardy to 0°F.

Parkinsonia aculeata

PENNISETUM setaceum (*P. ruppelii*). FOUNTAIN GRASS. Perennial grass. Mounding clumps of narrow, arching leaves produce 3- to 4-ft. stems tipped with showy, fuzzy coppery pink or purplish flower spikes. Useful in dry locations as relief in low ground cover plantings, among rocks and gravel. Cut spikes for arrangements before plants go to seed; seedlings can become pests. Best not to plant in rural areas where escape is likely. The variety 'Cupreum' has reddish brown leaves, dark plumes, does not self-sow. Hardy anywhere.

Pennisetum setaceum

PENSTEMON. Perennials or shrubby perennials. Widespread group (250 species and many hybrid strains) of North American plants of varied appearance, all with showy tubular flowers in a wide range of colors. Most are of western origin and tolerate capricious water supply; many are highly drought tolerant. Not widely available, but likely to become so with increasing awareness of water shortages. All like sun (light shade in hottest areas), excellent drainage. Most are short lived (3–4 years). Hybrids are more tolerant of ordinary garden water than species.

Penstemon heterophyllus purdyi

P. barbatus. Open, sprawling habit to 3 ft., with loose spikes of red flowers in early summer. Selections are available in pink and purple. Hardy to any cold, short lived in warm-winter areas.

P. heterophyllus purdyi. Upright or spreading, 1–2 ft. tall, with spikelike clusters of flowers in lavender to blue tones. 'Blue Bedder', pure blue, is a well known selection. Hardy to 10°–15°F.

P. pinifolius. Spreading shrublet 4–6 in. tall or rarely taller, with evergreen needlelike foliage and red 1½-in. flowers. Rock garden plant or small-scale ground cover. Hardy below 0°F.

PEROVSKIA atriplicifolia. RUSSIAN SAGE. Perennial. Many-stemmed plant to 3 ft. with gray green foliage finely cut and toothed and a haze of small lavender blue flowers in many-branched spiky clusters above the foliage. Long summer bloom if old flowering branches are cut off. Likes heat, sun, good drainage, winter chill. Hardy below 0°F.

Perovskia atriplicifolia

PHORMIUM tenax. NEW ZEALAND FLAX. Evergreen perennial. Many long, stiff, swordlike leaves arise from the base in fan pattern. Dull red or yellow flowers cluster on stalks that tower above foliage—more important for outline than color. Leaves of species can reach 9 ft. in length. Useful for bold effects. Grows in full sun or light shade. Takes heat, wind, drought, salt air, wet soil (but not in desert climates). Varieties with bronze or variegated foliage are usually smaller, less stiff, not so hardy. Withstands cold to around 10°–15°F.

Phormium tenax

PHYLA nodiflora (*Lippia repens*). LIPPIA. Perennial. Prostrate, forming flat mat of gray green leaves to ¾ in. long. Small white to pink flowers in tight, round ½-in. heads spring to fall. Useful low-water lawn substitute, but bees love it. Can take foot traffic and considerable drought when established, but dormant in winter. Looks better with some water and feeding. Hardy to 15°–20°F.

Phyla nodiflora

PINUS. PINE. Evergreen trees, rarely shrubs, characterized by having long, slender needles in bundles. Most are moderately to highly drought tolerant (with notable exception of most pines with 5 needles to the bundle); only a few of the most tolerant and adaptable can be dealt with here. All need good to excellent drainage and prefer clean, unpolluted air, little fertilizer. Check with local experts on best kinds to plant—or to avoid.

Pinus pinea

P. brutia (*P. halepensis brutia*). CALABRIAN PINE. Rapid growth to 30–80 ft., with dark green needles, fairly symmetrical form. Withstands heat, wind, ordinary soil, drought. Hardy to 0°F.

P. eldarica. AFGHAN PINE. Similar to *P. brutia* and may be a geographic race of that pine from Afghanistan and Pakistan. Excellent pine for desert, near coast. Hardy to around 0°F.

P. pinea. ITALIAN STONE PINE. Moderate growth rate to 40–80 ft., a globe in youth, later a broad-topped umbrella, eventually flat-topped. Eventually too large for small gardens, picturesque as roadside or skyline tree. Tolerates heat and drought. Hardy to around 0°F. when mature, more tender when young.

PISTACIA chinensis. CHINESE PISTACHE. Deciduous tree of moderate growth rate to 60 ft., gawky and irregular in youth, but eventually dense and shapely. Leaves divided featherwise into 2- to 4-in. leaflets. Outstanding fall foliage color—scarlet, red, orange, sometimes yellow. Small fruits on female trees bright red, aging dark blue. Needs staking and pruning when young, but worth the effort. Tolerates heat, wind, drought (but can take summer water), moderately alkaline soil. Hardy to 0°–10°F.

Pistacia chinensis

PITTOSPORUM tobira. Evergreen shrub. Dense, broad growth to 6–15 ft. Leathery, shiny dark green leaves 2–5 in. long. Clusters of creamy white flowers at branch ends in spring have scent of orange blossoms. 'Variegata' has leaves edged with white and is somewhat smaller. Both are useful as screens, hedges, or for massing in sun or light shade. Established plants can take much drought. Hardy to 10°F.

Pittosporum tobira

PLUMBAGO auriculata. CAPE PLUMBAGO. Semievergreen shrub or vine. Without support a broad, sprawling mound 6 ft. tall, 8–10 ft. wide. With support, a vine to 12 ft. Light to medium green leaves 1–2 in. long. Pale blue to white flowers 1 in. wide in rounded phloxlike clusters spring through autumn, all year in mildest areas. Ordinary soil, good drainage; tolerates heat, hottest sun, little water once established (slow to take off). Good background, screen, roadside shrub. Drops leaves in heavy frost, recovers fast; survives 20°F.

Plumbago auriculata

POTENTILLA fruticosa. Deciduous shrubs. Shrubby potentillas grow 2–5 ft. tall and equally wide, depending on variety. Leaves are divided fanwise into 3–7 leaflets and may be gray green or green on top, gray beneath. Flowers resemble little single roses from ¾ to 2 in. wide; season lasts June to October. Most are deep or pale yellow or white; some newer varieties are red or orange (but only in moderately cool weather). Plants tolerate heat, cold, poor soil, moderate drought, but need good drainage. Cut out a few of the oldest stems from time to time. Hardy well below 0°F.

Potentilla fruticosa

PROSOPIS. MESQUITE. Deciduous or evergreen trees with dark bark, spreading branches, leaves divided into tiny leaflets, tiny flowers in catkinlike spikes followed by flat seed pods. They hybridize freely, and names are much confused in nurseries. All endure heat, alkaline soil, and drought, but can tolerate lawn water. Valuable in desert or low rainfall areas of the Southwest.

P. alba. ARGENTINE MESQUITE. Vigorous, fast growing single-trunk tree with dense canopy of blue green foliage. Nearly evergreen; new leaves appear as old ones drop.

P. chilensis. CHILEAN MESQUITE. Two trees sold under this name. One, probably a hybrid, is deciduous, vigorous, with a spreading head of deep green foliage. The other, also vigorous, is less dense in the canopy, evergreen in mild winters, deciduous in cold-winter areas.

P. glandulosa. HONEY or TEXAS MESQUITE. Deciduous tree, often with multiple trunks. Bright green leaves, drooping branchlets. *P. g. torreyana* is native westward to California.

Prosopis glandulosa

P. velutina (*P. g. velutina*). ARIZONA MESQUITE. Arizona native, tending to be smaller and shrubbier than *P. glandulosa*.

PROTEA. Evergreen shrubs with large, showy heads of flowers surrounded by colorful bracts like colorful giant artichokes. Excellent cut flowers hold color a long time, will preserve form after drying. All need perfect drainage, full sun, protection from hot, dry winds. Most need acid soil. Young plants tender to cold. Feed lightly with nitrogen; avoid phosphorus, which can kill plants. Need moderate summer water until established, then water once every 2–4 weeks.

Protea cynaroides

P. cynaroides. KING PROTEA. Open, spreading plant to 3–5 ft. with long-stalked oval leaves, white flowers circled by pink to crimson bracts in 10- to 12-in. flower heads. Needs regular, infrequent watering throughout the year. Hardy to 25°–27°F.

P. neriifolia. Grows 10–12 ft. tall, 6–8 ft. wide, with narrow leaves like oleander and flower heads (autumn and winter) 5 in. long, 3 in. wide with pink to salmon bracts, black tipped. Can take alkaline soil. Hardy to 17°F.

PRUNUS. Deciduous and evergreen trees and shrubs comprising the stone fruits, many flowering deciduous trees and shrubs, and a few evergreen ornamental trees and shrubs. Many of the stone fruits can withstand some drought if planted in deep soil and deeply rooted, but the following ornamentals are reasonably drought resistant under ordinary garden conditions.

Prunus caroliniana

P. besseyi. WESTERN SAND CHERRY. Deciduous shrub 3–6 ft. tall, with white spring flowers followed by sweet black cherries to ¾ in. Useful for pies, jams, jellies. Can take heat, wind, drought, extreme cold (well below 0°F.).

P. caroliniana. CAROLINA LAUREL CHERRY. Evergreen shrub or tree to 35–40 ft., but easy to restrain by pruning or clipping as screen or hedge. Glossy green, smooth-edged 2- to 4-in. leaves, 1-in. spikes of white flowers followed by ½-in. (or smaller) black fruits. Average soil; tolerates heat, wind. Treat for chlorosis in alkaline soils. Compact varieties are 'Bright 'n Tight' and 'Compacta'. Hardy to 0°–10°F.

P. cistena. DWARF RED-LEAF PLUM. Deciduous shrub to 6–10 ft.; can be trained as small single-stem tree. Leaves are purple, flowers white to pinkish, fruit blackish purple. 'Big Cis' grows to 14 ft. tall, 12 ft. wide. Hardy well below 0°F.

P. ilicifolia. HOLLYLEAF CHERRY. Evergreen shrub or small tree to 20–30 ft. with rich, dark green leaves with spiny margins like holly. White spring flowers are in 3- to 6-in. spikes in spring. Reddish purple fruit to ¾ in. is edible, but largely pit. Needs good drainage in sun or light shade. Needs no summer water once established. Can be pruned as hedge or screen. Hardy to about 10°F.

P. lyonii. CATALINA CHERRY. Similar to *P. ilicifolia*, but larger (to 45 ft. tall), with larger (3- to 5-in. leaves) with smooth edges, larger black fruits. Leaves of younger plants may be toothed, and intermediate hybrids between the two evergreen cherries are common. Hardiness and uses same as for *P. ilicifolia*.

PUNICA granatum. POMEGRANATE. Deciduous shrub or small tree, usually multiple-trunked, to 10 ft. tall. Narrow, glossy bright green leaves turn bright yellow in fall. Orange red flowers 2–4 in. wide in early summer turn into globular red fruits in autumn, early winter. Needs summer heat to flower. Can tolerate extreme heat, alkaline soil. When established, will get by with little water, but needs adequate supply to produce fruit. Drought followed by heavy irrigation will cause fruit to split. Dwarf varieties with shallow root systems require more regular irrigation. Hardy to around 10°F.

Punica granatum

PYRACANTHA. FIRETHORN. Evergreen shrubs, generally thorny, with clustered white flowers and masses of showy red, orange, or yellow berrylike fruit. Many species, but most are offered as named varieties. Toughness, drought tolerance is attested by their propensity to volunteer along roads and uncultivated areas. Most are used as espaliers, barriers, rough hedges; some low growers are useful ground or bank covers. Control size and shape by pinching shoots and cutting back fruiting branches to a well placed side shoot.

Pyracantha coccinea

P. coccinea. Rounded bush to 10–12 ft. or more, with red orange berries. Hardiest pyracanthas are varieties 'Government Red' and 'Kasan' (red berries), and 'Lalandei Monrovia' (orange berries). Hardy except in very coldest parts of the country.

P. 'Mohave'. Shrub to 12 ft. tall and wide, with red berries. Hardy below 0°F.

P. 'Teton'. To 12 ft. tall, 4 ft. wide, with orange berries. Hardy well below 0°F.

QUERCUS. OAK. Deciduous or evergreen trees. Most are deep rooted and reasonably drought tolerant once established, but a few are outstandingly so. Nursery-grown trees or trees you raise yourself from acorns seldom pose cultural difficulties, but existing oaks you acquire with a property need special care. Avoid changing the soil level around them by cutting or filling, and keep the base of the trunk dry in regions where oak root fungus (*Armillariella mellea*) or other crown rot fungus is a problem.

Quercus macrocarpa

Q. agrifolia. COAST LIVE OAK. Round-headed, spreading evergreen tree 40–70 ft. tall, frequently broader. Native to Coast Ranges of California. Smooth, dark gray bark; open, graceful canopy of rounded, hollylike, 1- to 3-in. leaves. Cherished tree in the West in spite of greedy roots, heavy leaf drop in spring as new leaves emerge. Hardy to around 10°F.

Q. ilex. HOLLY OAK, HOLM OAK. Dense, round-headed, 40- to 70-ft.-tall evergreen tree with heavy, horizontally spreading limbs, 1½- to 3-in. leaves either smooth-edged or toothed. Native to Mediterranean regions. Stands seaside conditions well. Can be sheared into formal topiary shapes. Hardy to 0°F.

Q. macrocarpa. BUR OAK, MOSSY CUP OAK. Deciduous tree native to eastern and central U.S., Great Plains. To 60–75 ft. tall, eventually of equal or greater spread. Leaves 8–10 in. long, deeply lobed with rounded lobes. Big acorns sit in mossy, fringed cups. One of the hardiest oaks, to −30° to −40°F.

RHAMNUS. Evergreen or deciduous shrubs, rarely small trees, with inconspicuous flowers, berrylike fruit.

R. alaternus. ITALIAN BUCKTHORN. Evergreen shrub or small tree. Fast growth to 20 ft., spreading as wide, but easily kept narrow by close planting or shaping. Leaves bright shiny green, ¾–2 in. long. Fruit black, ¼ in. long, inconspicuous. Very fast growth makes it a good tall screen or (staked and trained) small evergreen tree.

Rhamnus alaternus

Easily sheared and shaped. Withstands heat, wind, drought, or regular watering. Takes full sun or light shade. Hardy to 0°F. 'Variegata' has white-edged leaves.

R. californica. COFFEEBERRY. Western native evergreen shrub to 15 ft. Dense growth, with 1- to 3-in. dark green to dull green leaves, large round inedible berries that turn from green to red, then black. 'Eve Case' (dense, compact, 4–8 ft. tall) and 'Seaview' (1½ ft. tall, 6–8 ft. wide) are selected forms. In warm areas looks best with occasional summer water. Grows well in sun or light shade. Hardy to 0°F.

R. frangula. ALDER BUCKTHORN. Deciduous shrub or small tree to 15–18 ft. with roundish, glossy dark green 1½- to 3-in. leaves, fruit ripening red to black. Best known form is *R. f.* 'Columnaris', TALLHEDGE BUCKTHORN, which grows 12–15 ft. tall, 4 ft. wide. Set 2½ ft. apart for a tight, narrow hedge 4–15 ft. tall. Needs some summer water. Hardy well below 0°F.

RHAPHIOLEPIS indica. INDIA HAWTHORN. Evergreen shrubs of compact habit 2–5 ft. tall, with glossy, leathery 1½- to 3-in. leaves and clusters of white to pink flowers at twig ends. Clusters of small dark blue berries follow. Among the most widely planted shrubs in the West and South. Easy in full sun, less compact and floriferous in light shade. Can take moderate drought or routine watering, occasional temperature drops to near 0°F. Among many fine garden varieties are 'Ballerina', 3 ft. by 3 ft.,

Rhaphiolepis indica

with soft pink flowers in spring, with some repeat bloom; and 'Snow White', 4 ft. by 4 ft., with white flowers.

RHUS. SUMAC. Evergreen or deciduous shrubs or trees. All tolerate drought and poor soil. All require good drainage.

R. glabra. SMOOTH SUMAC. Deciduous shrub to 10 ft. or a small tree to 20 ft. Spreads into thickets by underground roots. Fernlike leaves divided into many narrow, toothed leaflets 2–5 in. long. These turn from deep green to scarlet in fall.

Rhus typhina

Flowers are inconspicuous, but are followed by upright clusters of dark red fruit which adorn branch ends into winter. Hardy to −30 to −40°F.

R. lancea. AFRICAN SUMAC. Evergreen tree of slow growth to 25 ft., with rough, dark red bark, open, spreading branches, graceful weeping branchlets, and leaves with 3 willowlike leaflets 3–5 in. long. Pea-sized yellow or red fruit on female trees can pose a problem over pavement. Endures desert heat and drought, but can also thrive in lawns. Hardy to 12°F.

R. ovata. SUGAR BUSH. Evergreen shrub to 10 ft. tall, with glossy, leathery green leaves to 3 in. long. Small white to pinkish spring flowers are followed by small red, hairy fruit coated with a sugary secretion. Stands much heat and drought, but needs fall planting in desert—hard to start in great heat. Hardy to near 0°F.

R. typhina. STAGHORN SUMAC. Deciduous shrub or small tree to 15–30 ft. with sparse, regularly forking branches covered with short brown hairs like deer antlers in velvet. Resembles *R. glabra* otherwise. Variety 'Laciniata' has leaflets deeply cut, almost fernlike.

RIBES viburnifolium. CATALINA PERFUME, EVERGREEN CURRANT. Sprawling evergreen shrub to 3 ft. tall, 12 ft. wide, with arching or trailing stems that may root in moist soil. Leaves leathery, roundish, dark green, fragrant when rubbed against. (Some say scent is like pine, others like apple.) Inconspicuous pinkish flowers and red fruit. Excellent ground cover for sun near coast, part shade inland. Choice underplanting for native oaks where heavy watering is not safe. Hardy to 10°–15°F.

Ribes viburnifolium

ROBINIA. LOCUST. Deciduous trees or shrubs with leaves divided featherwise into many roundish leaflets and with hanging clusters of sweet pea–shaped flowers. All are hardy to practically any degree of cold or heat and can endure drought when established. They can thrive in poor soil. Only faults are suckering and brittle wood.

R. ambigua. Name given to hybrids between *R. pseudoacacia* and *R. viscosa,* a little-grown pink-flowered species. Best known variety is 'Idahoensis', to 40 ft., with magenta rose flowers in 8-in. clusters.

R. pseudoacacia. BLACK LOCUST. Fast growth to 75 ft. with open, sometimes gaunt branching pattern. Fragrant white flowers in 4- to 8-in. clusters turn into beanlike brown pods. This eastern U. S. native is tough enough to have gone native in many parts of the world, including California's gold country, where it exists with no summer water.

Robinia pseudoacacia

ROMNEYA coulteri. MATILIJA POPPY. Perennial. Native to Southern California and Baja California, this big, tough plant is hardy in all but the coldest parts of the country. Gray green stems clothed with gray green, deeply cut leaves grow to 8 ft. or more. White crepe-textured flowers with central mass of golden stamens can reach 9 in. in diameter. Bloom season May–July, longer if plants are irrigated. Spreads

Romneya coulteri

by underground rhizomes and can invade more delicate plantings. Needs sun, drainage. Tolerates many soil types, water regimes; withhold water to limit spread. Cut old stems nearly to ground in late winter for neatness.

ROSA. ROSE. A few wild roses, along with selections and hybrids from them, have low water requirements once established.

R. harisonii. HARISON'S YELLOW ROSE. Deciduous shrub to 6–8 ft., forming thickets of thorny stems with fine-textured foliage and abundant semidouble, bright yellow, fragrant flowers in late spring, sometimes reblooming in fall where climate is mild. Old pioneer's variety, often persisting around old farm houses. Hardy anywhere.

Rosa harisonii

R. rugosa. Deciduous shrubs from 3–8 ft. tall according to variety, with prickly stems and shining, crinkled-seeming leaves. Flowers are 3–4 in. across, single, semidouble, or double, fragrant, white and cream through pink, deep red, and purple. Showy inch-wide fruits can be used in preserves. Resistant to wind, salt breeze, drought when established. Hardy anywhere.

ROSMARINUS officinalis. ROSEMARY. Evergreen shrub with narrow, crowded, aromatic leaves that are shiny dark green above, grayish white underneath. Light lavender blue flowers ¼–½ in. long make a show in winter and spring. Leaves are used as seasoning herb. Named varieties may be prostrate and useful as ground cover ('Lockwood de Forest', 'Prostratus'); erect and to 6 ft. tall ('Tuscan Blue'), or intermediate ('Collingwood Ingram', with bright blue flowers). Needs good drainage; tolerates heat, poor soil, drought. Excess water stimulates excess growth. Hardy to near 0°F.

Rosmarinus officinalis

RUDBECKIA hirta. GLORIOSA DAISY, BLACK EYED SUSAN. Short lived perennials, biennials. Upright, branching plants with rough, hairy stems and leaves. Wild plants (black-eyed Susans) have single 3- to 4-in. daisies with orange yellow rays, black purple centers. Improved garden strains (Gloriosa daisies) with 5- to 7-in. flowers in shades of yellow, orange, or mahogany, often with contrasting bands or zones. All give long bloom during hot weather and usually seed abundantly. They need sun, good drainage, enough water to get started. Hardy anywhere.

Rudbeckia hirta

RUTA graveolens. RUE. Perennial. Upright, dense growth to 2–3 ft. with finely cut blue green leaves, flattish clusters of greenish yellow flowers followed by brown seed pods. Plant has an odd odor when brushed against; some people like it, some don't. Grown in herb collections more for legend than for use. 'Jackman's Blue' has fine gray blue foliage. Hardy anywhere.

Ruta graveolens

SALVIA. SAGE. Perennials and shrubby perennials. Widely varied group of more than 750 species, including common garden annuals, an herb for seasoning, and a number of perennials and shrubby perennials. Most have scented foliage and all have flowers arranged in elongated spike-like clusters. Many are native to dry climates; a few of the more widely grown kinds are listed below. These need full sun or very light shade, excellent drainage; they can get along with little or no summer water. Plants withstand occasional drops into the low 20s.

Salvia leucantha

New species and selections are entering the nursery trade in large numbers, especially in California and the Southwest. Check your best nurseryman for new kinds.

S. clevelandii. Evergreen shrub to 4 ft., with gray green leaves and blue flowers May–August. Powerful, pleasant fragrance.

S. greggii. Erect, bushy plant 3–4 ft. tall with medium green ½- to 1-in. leaves and clusters of red flowers in late spring and summer (fall through spring in the desert). Pink, white, and coral color forms are widely available.

S. leucantha. MEXICAN BUSH SAGE. Graceful evergreen shrub to 3–4 ft. tall, equally wide. Long, leaning or arching velvety purple spikes with small white flowers bloom summer through fall. Cut faded stems to ground; new ones will replace them.

SANTOLINA. Evergreen herbs or subshrubs with very finely divided foliage, dense habit improved by some clipping and shaping, and individually tiny flowers that are showy in the mass if not cut off in shearing. Tough, undemanding plants which like sun and need no summer water where summers are cool. Hardy anywhere.

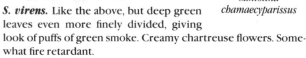

S. chamaecyparissus. LAVENDER COTTON. To 2 ft. tall, best clipped to 1 ft. or less. Whitish gray foliage, yellow flowers. Use as edging, ground cover.

S. virens. Like the above, but deep green leaves even more finely divided, giving look of puffs of green smoke. Creamy chartreuse flowers. Somewhat fire retardant.

Santolina chamaecyparissus

SCHINUS molle. CALIFORNIA PEPPER TREE. Evergreen tree 25–40 ft. tall, equally wide. Old trees have heavy, gnarled trunks with wide-spreading branches, gracefully weeping branchlets bearing bright green leaves divided featherwise into many narrow 1½- to 2-in.-long leaflets. Inconspicuous flowers are followed in fall and winter by drooping clusters of rose red berries. Unquestionably attractive if given enough room, but not a tree for narrow parking strips.

Not universally loved; greedy root systems, litter, and susceptibility to scale are problems. Tolerates desert heat, low water, poor soil. Hardy to around 15°F.

Schinus molle

SEDUM. Succulent perennials or subshrubs of widely varying sizes, degrees of hardiness, and garden uses. Most widely used are low growing ground cover species. Fleshy leaves are good at hoarding water; plants need little summer irrigation. Useful, fast spreading ground cover in sun or partial shade, but cannot take foot traffic. Easy to propagate; any fragment will take root.

Sedum spathulifolium

S. acre. GOLDMOSS SEDUM. Evergreen, 2–5 in. tall, with upright stems arising from trailing, rooting stems. Leaves cylindrical, tiny, light green. Spring flowers are yellow. Hardy anywhere. Useful between stepping-stones, in dry walls; can become invasive. Hardy anywhere.

S. spathulifolium. Blue green fleshy leaves in tight rosettes. Needs no water in cool-summer areas.

SENECIO. Widely varied plants related to daisies; annuals, perennials, shrubs, vines, succulents, some weeds. Drought-tolerant kinds include perennials and succulents.

S. cineraria. DUSTY MILLER. One of several plants so named. Shrubby perennial 2–2½ ft. tall, with woolly white leaves cut into blunt-tipped lobes. Flowers yellow or creamy yellow, often cut off to maintain mounded form of plant. Prune occasionally to keep compact. Use for contrast with green foliage and bright flowers. Needs little water; hardy except in coldest regions, where it needs protection.

Senecio cineraria

S. mandraliscae (*Kleinia mandraliscae*). Succulent perennial 1½–2 ft. tall. Leaves cylindrical, slightly curved, 3–3½ in. long, strikingly blue gray in color. Use in pattern planting for foliage color. Hardy to about 20°F.

SOLANDRA maxima. CUP-OF-GOLD VINE. Evergreen vine. Fast grower to 40 ft., with thick stems and broad, glossy leaves 4–6 in. long. Needs fastening to its support (or can be clipped as a coarse hedge). Bowl-shaped yellow flowers striped with brownish purple are 6–8 in. across. Blooms early spring, with some repeats. Endures ocean wind, fog, heat (but needs shaded roots in hot areas). Tender to frost; give protection overhead where frosts occur. Needs little water once woody framework and sturdy root system are established.

Solandra maxima

SOLANUM jasminoides. POTATO VINE. Evergreen vine, deciduous or partly so in colder winters. Fast growth by twining stems. Medium green 1½- to 3-in. leaves, white flowers 1 in. wide in clusters of 8–12. Bloom nearly continuous, heaviest in spring. Use to cover fence, trellis, arbor. Prune heavily from time to time to control tangle, stimulate new growth. Looks best with at least a monthly watering. Hardy to about 20°F.

Solanum jasminoides

SOLLYA heterophylla. AUSTRALIAN BLUEBELL CREEPER. Evergreen shrub or vine. Grows 2–3 ft. tall, somewhat wider as a loose, spreading shrub, to 6–8 ft. with support as a vine. Glossy, shiny, bright green 1- to 2-in. narrow leaves, long show of bright blue ½-in. flowers in clusters throughout summer. Needs good drainage, full sun near coast, part shade in hotter regions. Established plants need little water, but are better looking with regular watering. Can grow under eucalyptus trees. Fine bank or ground cover. Hardy to around 20°F.

Sollya heterophylla

SOPHORA secundiflora. Evergreen shrub; can be trained into a 25-ft. tree with narrow crown, upright branches. Very slow growth. Leaves 4–6 in. long, divided into glossy, dark green 1- to 2-in. leaflets.

Inch-wide, sweet-scented violet blue flowers in wisterialike clusters appear in spring. Silvery gray seedpods split upon ripening to show scarlet ½-in. seeds, showy but very poisonous; remove faded flowers before seeds form. Tolerates desert heat and alkaline soil, but needs good drainage and occasional water. Hardy to 10°–15°F.

Sophora secundiflora

STACHYS byzantina (S. lanata, S. olympica). LAMB'S EARS. Perennial with soft, thick, white-woolly tongue-shaped leaves on spreading stems. Flower stalks with small purplish flowers in summer do not improve plant's appearance and are better cut off as they appear. A non-flowering variety occasionally seen is 'Silver Carpet'.

Use as edging or ground cover to contrast with green foliage or to set off brilliant colors. Average soil, sun or light shade, good drainage, little water. Hardy anywhere, but looks tired after cold or wet winters; cut back to rejuvenate.

Stachys byzantina

SYMPHORICARPOS. Deciduous shrubs noted for tolerance of drought, poor soil, shade, city air. Small white or pinkish flowers are followed by ornamental white or pink fruit. Used as coarse ground cover, erosion control on banks.

S. albus. COMMON SNOWBERRY. Spreading or upright shrub 2–6 ft. tall. Pink flowers followed by white, ½-in. fruit that lasts late summer into winter. Fruit production best in sun. Hardy anywhere.

S. mollis. CREEPING SNOWBERRY. Like the above but grows 1½ ft. tall, more spreading habit, less fruit. Hardy to −10°F.

S. orbiculatus (S. vulgaris). CORAL BERRY, INDIAN CURRANT. Like C. albus, but with profusion of small purplish red fruits. Showy fall and into winter. Hardy anywhere.

Symphoricarpos albus

TAMARIX. TAMARISK. Deciduous or evergreen shrubs or trees with tiny leaves and clouds of tiny flowers that make masses of pink (usually) or white foam at bloom time. Tough plants that endure desert heat and alkaline soil, survive drought by deep and extensive root systems (which make them risky choices for small gardens with choice plants). Names of species are almost hopelessly mixed up, and exact identification is difficult. All are easy to propagate by cuttings set in place and watered. The following are most widely seen:

Tamarix ramosissima

T. aphylla (T. articulata). ATHEL TREE. Tree of very fast growth to 30–50 ft., with greenish jointed branches that give look of an evergreen. White to pink flowers in late summer are less showy than those of other species. Useful windbreak in desert. Roots extremely competitive. Damaged at 0°F., but comes back fast from injury.

T. parviflora (often sold as T. tetrandra or T. africana). Shrub to 6–15 ft. Airy, arching branches covered in spring with pink flowers which later turn brown. Cut back after bloom to groom and limit growth. Hardy anywhere.

T. chinensis (T. pentandra, T. juniperina, T. ramosissima). SALT CEDAR. Blooms spring, summer, or fall, with flowers that may be white, cream, pink, or purple. Looks best cut to ground every spring to remain a 6- to 12-ft. shrub. Untrained, a 20- to 30-ft. shrub with greedy root system that steals water from other plants. A weed in some parts of the Southwest. Hardy anywhere.

TAXUS. YEW. Evergreen trees or shrubs with short, flat, dark green needlelike foliage and (on female plants) bright red fleshy fruits containing a black seed. Fruit and foliage both poisonous. Slow growing, long lived choice landscape plants that accept regular garden watering but tolerate infrequent irrigation when well established. Easily shaped or sheared and tolerant of average garden soils. Suffer from reflected sun in hot weather, or from winter sunshine when soil is frozen around roots. Protect from vine weevils, scale, mites.

Taxus baccata

T. baccata. ENGLISH YEW. Best known for its garden varieties. 'Stricta' ('Fastigiata'), IRISH YEW, grows slowly into a column 20 ft. or more in height, with crowded upright branches that tend to spread toward the top. Tie them together with wire to maintain narrow outline. Choice plant for vertical effect against walls, screening, background planting. 'Repandens' makes a 2-ft., wide-spreading ground cover. There are golden-leafed forms of both spreading and upright yew. Hardy to around 0°–10°F.

T. cuspidata. JAPANESE YEW. Hardier to cold, surviving in shaded Rocky Mountain gardens, but not satisfactory in mild-winter areas. 'Capitata' is a dense cone of slow growth to 10–25 ft. 'Nana' to 3 ft. tall, 6 ft. wide in 20 years, is a good low barrier or hedge.

T. media. Hybrids between the two previous species. 'Brownii' (4–8 ft.), 'Hatfieldii' (10–12 ft.), and 'Hicksii' (10–12 ft. and narrow) are all useful for screen or hedge.

TECOMA stans (Stenolobium stans).
YELLOW BELLS, YELLOW TRUMPET
FLOWER, YELLOW ELDER. Evergreen large
shrub or small tree. Trainable as tree in
mildest winter areas; may die back considerably in frost, but recovers quickly, grows
fast. Leaves divided into toothed, 1½- to
4-in. leaflets. Bright yellow, bell-shaped 2-
in. flowers in large clusters bloom June to
January. *T. s. angustata*, with narrow leaflets, is best adapted to desert heat, needs
less water. Hardy to 20°–25°F.

Tecoma stans

**TECOMARIA capensis (Tecoma ca-
pensis).** CAPE HONEYSUCKLE. Evergreen vine or shrub. Can be pruned as a 6-
to 8-ft. shrub or hedge or, with support,
trained as a 15- to 25-ft. vine. Leaves shiny
dark green and divided into many leaflets.
Clusters of orange red, 2-in. tubular flowers bloom October through winter. 'Au-
rea' has yellow flowers. Endures sun, heat,
wind (including ocean wind), and light
shade. Use as bank cover, espalier, rough hedge or screen. Hardy
to around 25°F.

Tecomaria capensis

TEUCRIUM. Shrubs or subshrubs in the
mint family. Tough plants for hot, dry, rocky
situations.

T. chamaedrys. GERMANDER. Grows 1 ft.
tall, 2 ft. wide, with many upright stems
thickly set with toothed, shiny, dark green
leaves ¾ in. long. Flower spikes in summer
are red purple or white. Shear as low edging, border, clipped hedge, small-scale
ground cover. Hardy anywhere, and can
take ordinary watering in well drained soil.

*Teucrium
chamaedrys*

T. fruticans. BUSH GERMANDER. Open,
airy, silvery-stemmed shrub 4–8 ft. tall and
as wide or wider. Leaves 1¼ in. long, sil-
very gray. Lavender blue flowers in spikes form at branch ends
through most of the year. Thin and cut back in late winter or
early spring. Use as informal, unclipped hedge or shear for more
formal effect. Avoid overwatering. Hardy to 10°–15°F.

THYMUS. THYME. Perennials or subshrubs, most with aromatic leaves. Give
them light, fast draining soil, full sun or
lightest shade in hot regions. They require
far less water than lawn or most other
ground covers, but will need occasional
irrigation where summers are hot and
rainless. Hardy anywhere.

*Thymus praecox
arcticus*

**T. praecox arcticus (T. serpyllum, T. dru-
cei).** MOTHER-OF-THYME. Mat-forming
ground cover with creeping stems and
upright branches 2–6 in. tall, with ¼-in.
roundish, dark green, aromatic leaves.
Clustered tiny purplish flowers appear June–September. 'Albus'
has white flowers, 'Coccineus' and 'Reiter's' dark red. Use as
small-scale ground cover, between stones or bricks in paving, as
miniature lawns. Leaves useful in seasoning.

T. pseudolanuginosus (T. lanuginosus). WOOLLY THYME. Flat
or undulating gray green, furry mat that seldom shows its pink
flowers. Leaves essentially scentless.

T. vulgaris. COMMON THYME. Shrubby perennial 6–12 in. tall.
Leaves narrow to oval, ¼ in. long, gray green and fragrant. Tiny
lilac flowers in summer. Leaves are the classical seasoning thyme.
Use in herb garden, or as low edging.

TRISTANIA conferta. BRISBANE BOX.
Evergreen tree 30–60 ft. tall, upright,
eventually with a broad, spreading head.
Reddish brown bark peels away to show
smooth, light-colored new bark underneath. Leaves oval, leathery, glossy bright
green, 4–6 in. long. Fringed white to cream
¾-in. summer flowers resemble snow-
flakes. 'Variegata' has yellow leaf markings.
Needs water to get established, then quite
drought tolerant. Hardy to 26°F.

Tristania conferta

VERBENA. Perennials, some grown as annuals. Heat- and sun-loving plants that require good drainage and dry foliage. They
endure considerable drought and are useful in providing bright summer-long color
in parking strips, along driveways, on banks
and hillsides.

V. gooddingii. Perennial to 1½ ft. tall and
spreading, with deeply cut leaves and
pinkish lavender heads of flowers. Can grow
as an annual; sow in early spring for summer bloom. Reseeds if moisture is available. Hardy anywhere.

Verbena rigida

V. peruviana (V. chamaedryoides). PERU-
VIAN VERBENA. Perennial, sometimes
grown as an annual, forming flat mats of
closely set small leaves topped by flat-topped flower clusters.
Effect is that of a sheet of color. Scarlet in the original species;
red, pink, rose, purplish and white varieties exist. Hardy to
mid-20s.

V. rigida (V. venosa). Perennial (sometimes grown as an annual)
of spreading habit, 10–20 in. tall. Strongly toothed, 2- to 4-in.
rough dark green leaves are finely cut. Lilac to purple blue
flowers in cylindrical clusters on tall, stiff stems summer and fall.
Endures considerable drought. Blooms in 4 months when planted
from seed.

VIBURNUM lantana. WAYFARING TREE.
Deciduous shrub or small tree. Grows 8–
15 ft. tall, with broadly oval 5-in. downy
leaves that turn red in the fall. Clustered
tiny white flowers in May and June followed by showy scarlet fruit eventually
turning black. The variety 'Mohican' grows
to a compact 6 ft. tall, 8 ft. wide, and has
fruit that remains orange red. Sun or shade.
Withstands moderate drought, cold to
−40°F.

Viburnum lantana

VITIS vinifera. WINE GRAPE. Deciduous vine of indefinite size,
depending on age and training. Trunk and branches give strong

winter pattern, and fast growing canes can provide shade overhead or pattern against a wall. Autumn leaf color (yellow to deep burgundy) is a bonus, as are the grapes, which are produced abundantly if proper pruning is done. Established, deeply rooted vines can withstand long dry periods, cold to about 5°F.

Vitis vinifera

WESTRINGIA rosmariniformis. Evergreen shrub of spreading, open form 3–6 ft. tall, half again as wide. Leaves medium green to gray green above, white beneath; effect paler, airier than rosemary. Small white flowers in spring, all year in mildest areas. Needs little water, but can take routine garden irrigation. Wind resistant. Hardy to around 25°F.

Westringia rosmariniformis

WISTERIA. Deciduous vines capable of reaching huge size, but controllable enough to grow as small standard trees or big shrubs. Climbs by twining. Long leaves are divided featherwise into many leaflets. Violet blue flowers in long clusters make a grand show in spring. Plants are deep rooted and can withstand summer-long drought if necessary, but young plants need feeding and watering to get a good start. Hardy anywhere, but flower buds may be damaged in coldest areas.

W. floribunda. JAPANESE WISTERIA. Flower clusters 1½ ft. long (more in some varieties), violet blue, fragrant, opening gradually from base to tip of cluster.

Wisteria sinensis

W. sinensis. CHINESE WISTERIA. Blooms before leaves in April–May, with shorter clusters than Japanese wisteria. Blooms tend to open all at once for a magnificent show. Will take sun or considerable shade. There is a white variety.

XYLOSMA congestum (X. senticosum). Evergreen or deciduous shrub or small tree. Loose, graceful, spreading shrub 8–10 ft. tall and as wide or wider. Leaves are clean, shiny yellowish green. New growth is bronzy. Flowers and fruit inconspicuous. Main stem angles slowly upward if not staked, and side branches arch outward and downward, sometimes lying on the ground. Habit ideal for espalier or informal screen or hedge. Can be clipped or pruned into a formal hedge or staked to a single stem and made into a small single or multiple-stemmed tree. Needs little water, but looks better with some irrigation. Hardy to 10°F, but deciduous in hard frosts, recovering foliage quickly.

Xylosma congestum

YUCCA. Evergreen perennials, shrublike plants, or trees, all with tough, swordlike leaves in rosettes and large clusters of white or creamy flowers. Most are drought resistant; many are desert plants. Here are a few of the better-known species:

Y. aloifolia. SPANISH BAYONET. Slow grower to 10 ft. or more, with single or branched trunk, leaves to 2½ ft. long, 2 in. wide. White flowers 4 in. wide in 2-ft. erect clusters, summer. Keep away from walkways where sharp leaf tips could injure strollers. Hardy to around 10°F.

Y. filamentosa. Stemless, with stiff, narrow 2½-ft. leaves, tall, narrow clusters of white flowers to 4–7 ft. Hardy anywhere.

Y. flaccida. Similar to *Y. filamentosa*, but with broader, less stiff leaves and fatter flower clusters. Hardy anywhere, but does not thrive in desert climates.

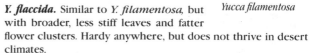

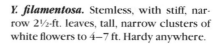

Yucca filamentosa

Y. gloriosa. SPANISH DAGGER, SOFT-TIP YUCCA. Much like *Y. aloifolia*, but with soft, innocuous leaf tips.

Y. recurvifolia (*Y. pendula*). Single-trunked or lightly branched with age, to 10 ft., with 2- to 3-ft. leaves 2 in. wide. Bluish gray green leaves are bent downward, and spiny tips bend to touch, are harmless. Large white flowers in open 3- to 5-ft. clusters, early summer.

ZAUSCHNERIA. CALIFORNIA FUCHSIA, HUMMINGBIRD FLOWER. Perennials, sometimes slightly shrubby. Can endure summer-long drought and still produce flowers summer through fall. Spreads freely by underground rhizomes and can invade other plantings. Use in native plant gardens, banks, out-of-the-way areas. All have narrow gray or green ½- to 1½-in. leaves and tubular 1½- to 2-in.-long scarlet flowers. Hardy to 0°F. (Some botanists consider these plants to be *Epilobium*, not *Zauschneria*).

Zauschneria californica

Z. californica. Stems erect or arching, 1–2 ft. tall. Evergreen in mild-winter climates. White forms exist.

Z. c. latifolia (*Z. septentrionalis*, often sold as *Z. latifolia* 'Etteri'). Perennial that makes 6-in. mats that die to the ground in winter. 'Solidarity Pink' is a pink variety.

Z. cana. Sprawling, woody-based stems carry narrow, silvery foliage. Evergreen in mild climates.

ZIZIPHUS jujuba. CHINESE JUJUBE, CHINESE DATE. Deciduous tree of slow to moderate growth to 20–30 ft., with gnarled branches and pendulous branchlets. Leaves glossy bright green, 1–2 in. long, with 3 prominent veins running base to tip. They turn bright yellow in fall. Prune in winter to shape or to encourage weeping habit. Inconspicuous early summer flowers are followed by date-sized, date-shaped brownish red fruit with a flavor similar to that of a dried apple. Fruit can be preserved in syrup, taking on a date flavor.

Ziziphus jujuba

Tree is resistant to drought, heat, and alkaline soil, but grows better in good garden conditions. Fruit on cultivated varieties can reach 2 in. in length. Hardy to 0°F., but fruit forms only where summers are long and warm.

General Subject Index

Plant Index